Who Should Read This Book

This book is not just for Jewish people. It is for anyone who is open to recovery-oriented teachings that can be gleaned from the Bible and the teachings of Jewish tradition.

✔ People who want to enrich their understanding of the Twelve Steps with Bible-based teachings

✔ Everyone facing the struggles of daily living who looks for insight and guidance from the Bible as a source of faith, strength, hope, and spiritual wisdom

✔ People in Twelve Step recovery programs

✔ Alcoholics and addicts, compulsive gamblers, those with eating disorders and sexaholics—and those who care about them

✔ Individuals who seek an authentic spiritual foundation for spiritual living based in sacred texts

✔ Rabbis, priests, and ministers—clergy who want to counsel congregants and parishioners spiritually

✔ Psychiatrists, psychologists, therapists providing religious meaning in the counseling context

✔ Codependents who live in or grew up in a dysfunctional family

✔ Jews and non-Jews from all walks of life

✔ Jews whose spiritual awakening might lead them to take a fresh, adult look at the religion of their birth

✔ All people who read *Twelve Jewish Steps to Recovery: A Personal Guide for Turning from Alcoholism and Other Addictions* (Jewish Lights Publishing, 1991)

Renewed Each Day

Daily Twelve Step Recovery Meditations Based on the Bible

Volume II
Leviticus, Numbers & Deuteronomy

Rabbi Kerry M. Olitzky
&
Aaron Z.

Foreword by **Sharon M. Strassfeld**
Afterword by **Rabbi Harold M. Schulweis**

Renewed Each Day: Daily Twelve Step Recovery Meditations Based On
The Bible, Volume II: Leviticus, Numbers & Deuteronomy.
copyright ©1992 by Kerry M. Olitzky and Aaron Z.

Library of Congress Cataloging-in-Publication Data

Olitzky, Kerry M., 1954–
   Renewed each day: daily twelve step recovery meditations based on
the Bible, v. 2: Leviticus, Numbers & Deuteronomy / Kerry M. Olitzky
& Aaron Z.

     1. Twelve-step programs—Religious aspects—Judaism—Meditations.
2. Bible. O.T. Pentateuch—Meditations. 3. Compulsive behavior—
Religious aspects—Judaism. 4. Substance abuse—Religious
aspects—Judaism. I. Z., Aaron, 1954– II. Title.

BM538.T85045 1992
296.7'2—dc20   92-8517
                                                     CIP

ISBN 1-879045-13-3

First edition
10 9 8 7 6 5 4 3 2 1

Manufactured in the United States of America

Published by JEWISH LIGHTS Publishing
A Division of LongHill Partners, Inc.
P.O. Box 237
Sunset Farm Offices, Route 4
Woodstock, Vermont 05091
Tel: (802) 457-4000
Fax: (802) 457-4004

For Sheryl, Avi, and Jesse, for living Torah so that I may learn it.

KERRY M. OLITZKY

To my wise-hearted wife, Elaine, you angel you . . .

AARON Z.

Contents

Volume I

Genesis

Exodus

Volume II

Leviticus

Numbers

Deuteronomy

Acknowledgments

If you believe as we do in the Yiddish notion of *bashert* (things just happen), then the bringing together of two people to prepare these volumes happened according to a plan whose comprehension is beyond us. Certain things are just meant to be. Hence, two authors from different walks of life came together to teach Torah and recovery because of a mutual interest in helping people in recovery on their spiritual journey. But no book is the sole work of any two individuals. There are many people whose words are spoken through our voices and who deserve our recognition and thanks.

To colleagues and friends at Hebrew Union College-Jewish Institute of Religion who constantly offer support and encouragement, I express my abiding gratitude. In particular, I mention Rabbi Alfred Gottschalk, president; Rabbi Paul Steinberg, vice president and dean of faculty; and Rabbi Norman Cohen, dean. These men are truly teachers of Torah and provide me with Torah wisdom each day.

While words are inadequate, I also thank my family. In my wife, Sheryl, God truly created for me a sheltering angel who is my life. The young, innocent interest and pride expressed by our children, Avi and Jesse Olitzky, buoy my efforts and instill my words and acts with ultimate meaning.

RABBI KERRY M. OLITZKY
Hebrew Union College–
Jewish Institute of Religion, NY

To Rabbi Jeff, for keeping Torah "green" for me; my sponsor, Bob, for his warmth, wisdom, and healing laughter; friends and supporters of the "Nyecker Rebbe"; JACS buddies Fran, Larry, Ephraim, and Shlomo; old friends Jeff, Austin, and Alan W., who were there in the beginning; fellowship friends Paul, Alan, Steve O., Mike M., and all those I haven't yet met—it does work; my brother Jed, a co-survivor; my children, Yosef, Eliahu, and Milke Rivke Yehudit, three blessings beyond my wildest dreams; and, last and first, the Holy Presence, for miracles and blessings both known and hidden, the gifts of Torah and recovery, and for renewing creation this day.

AARON Z.

Acknowledgments

All of the folks at Jewish Lights truly help fill the world with light. Publishers Stuart and Antoinette Matlins make the creation of a book a holy task. Likewise do Jevin Eagle and Carol Gersten provide direction and purpose to our work. And to our editor, Sara Brzowsky, whose insightful pen illuminated our every word, we offer thanks.

We also want to express our appreciation to those who shared their thoughts and joined them with our own: Rabbis Neil Gillman, Lawrence Hoffman, and Harold Schulweis, Danny Siegel and Dr. Ben Zion Twerski. And to those individuals and organizations who graciously allowed us to include their prayers and insights, we give voice to an abiding gratitude: Rabbi Lionel Blue and the Reform Synagogues of Great Britain, Rabbi Sidney Greenberg and Prayer Book Press, Rabbi Jules Harlow and the Rabbinical Assembly, Rabbi Zalman Schacter-Shalomi and the P'nai Or Fellowship, and Joseph Yordan and the JACS Foundation.

KERRY M. OLITZKY & AARON Z.

Foreword

The thing we know as Jews with absolute certainty is this: God has spoken to us and continues to speak to us through the Word found in our holy texts. We understand that there is an encounter that takes place in the presence of the text, whether in prayer or study, that cannot be achieved by Jews in any other manner. For this reason, we have come to prize the study of Torah, understanding that Torah is our link to understanding who we are, where we come from, and the direction in which we travel.

Rabbi Zalman Schachter-Shalomi teaches us to understand this through the *"mashal"* (the analogy) of driving a car. It is not possible, teaches Reb Zalman, to drive a car safely by only staring ahead at what we see through the windshield. We need to use the rear view mirror to constantly check ourselves and our own progress against what has been happening behind us, too. So too, our progress as Jews. We cannot come to understand God's world and our own place in it by constantly moving forward. We need to check in with where we came from and what our sources are, in order to move forward.

As Jews, we can check both forward and backward by studying each day—by rooting our day's beginning or end with a dip into the text. The text serves as the blueprint for the community. It is the sacred vessel that contains all the threads, all the fragments, all the liquid of our own understanding of who we are as Jews.

One final thing needs to be mentioned here.

Julius Lester wrote the following in his autobiographical work entitled *Lovesong* (published by Holt, 1988):

> In the winter of 1974, while on retreat at the Trappist monastery in Spencer, Massachusetts, one of the monks told me, "When you know the name by which God knows you, you will know who you are."

I searched for that name with the passion of one seeking the Eternal Beloved. I called myself Father, Writer, Teacher, but God did not answer.

Now I know the name by which God calls me. I am Yaakov *Daniel ben Avraham v'Sarah*.

I have become who I am. I am who I always was. I am no longer deceived by the black face which stares at me from the mirror.

I am Jew.

Knowing who we are. Reclaiming our community.

Once a religious member of my husband's family visited us at our new home. He looked around admiringly and commented "You have a lovely home. Did you *yarshan* it?" I looked puzzled at his use of the word *yarshan*. I know both Hebrew and Yiddish, yet I had never heard the term before. He realized my puzzlement and explained, "You know, *yarshan*—inherit!"

Over the years I've thought about his question, "Did you *yarshan* it?" The answer was, no, I didn't, but then I've thought to myself, "What exactly is it that I have *yarshaned* in my life?"

My answers to the question have changed as I've gotten older. One of the answers that has never changed for me is that I've *yarshaned* my link with my people. This is what I am entitled to for having been born to this people, and I claim this inheritance every day of my life. Indeed, I am constantly amazed at the Jews I meet who don't claim this inheritance. It is there— in all its glorious potentiality—waiting for us to move forward and assert our rights to it. It can't be bought; it can only be acquired through our own free choice.

Of course it can be scary to move back into a world we've left. Or to move forward into a world we've never been a part of. But we cheat ourselves when we deprive ourselves of the presence of the Jewish community in our lives.

The notion of feeling that I am "home" has always been an

important part of my internal consciousness. More often than not, I gauge a moment in my life by whether it feels like a good place for me to be—a healthy, healing place—or a place that isn't healthy, that doesn't feel like "home."

Such was my experience the first time I visited Havurat Shalom in Boston. It was a Friday evening, and I had been directed to the yellow building on College Avenue where *Kabbalat Shabbat* (welcoming the Sabbath) services would begin at 6 p.m. I arrived on time and walked into the strangest Jewish scene I had ever encountered. The prayer room was devoid of furniture and cushions lay scattered about the floor. A wicker ark hung on the wall with candles burning nearby. Absolute silence reigned among the people sitting on cushions on the floor. I gingerly perched myself on a cushion in the corner of the room and settled into that silence. After a time someone began to sing a *niggun*, a haunting melody with no words. I joined in and the thought that would come to serve as my gauge always afterward entered my mind for the first time: "This is my home."

My prayer for you who hold this book in your hands right now is that you grow to find your own home. And that it be the will of the *Ribbono Shel Olam*, the Master of the Universe, that you find that home in the Jewish community.

SHARON M. STRASSFELD

Introduction

My name is Aaron, and I'm a Jewish addict.

I am also married, a father of three children, a New York-area homeowner, over-educated, self-employed, frequently funny, thirtysomething, from the Bronx, a longtime Mets, Bob Dylan, and Grateful Dead fan, a voracious reader, and a whole lot of other semi-interesting stuff. But, for the purpose of this book, the main thing you need to know about me is that I'm a Jewish addict.

As a Jew, I am affiliated with an egalitarian Conservative synagogue in the New York metropolitan area. I had a Modern Orthodox upbringing, but my parents could not afford to send me to yeshiva. I did attend Yeshiva University's "beginner program" for two years but then transferred to a city college as drugs, sex, and rock 'n' roll seduced me away from the initial—and genuine—spiritual awakening that had led me to Yeshiva. I consider myself a Sabbath observer and keep a kosher home. I attend Shabbat services regularly but late. I am active in my synagogue's Men's Club, particularly with regard to Sunday morning softball and the yearly Super Bowl deli-laden bash. I don't wear *tzitzit* or a yarmulke, but my youngest son does. My two school-age children both attend a very *heimishe* Modern Orthodox day school. We celebrate all the Jewish holidays, read the Jewish newspapers, support Jewish causes, attend Jewish-topic lectures of interest, and have an extensive Jewish home library, as my wife and I are major book-lovers.

All this is to say that, as a Jew, I consider myself to be fairly normal. If anything, I am probably more knowledgeable and more observant than most in the American Jewish community.

And I am just as firmly and unmistakably an addict. I can more easily tell you how I became Jewish than why I became an addict—I was born Jewish. I don't quite know why I became an addict. Oh sure, I could spend a few pages reviewing childhood shame and self-esteem issues. I could talk about the sixties and how drugs were more socially and even spiritually acceptable then, but the fact is that a lot of people weaned themselves off drugs, and I kept right on going. I could even talk about how ours is a "quick-fix" culture and how many forces in our society conspire to make us feel "less than," but the fact is that we are all exposed, to some degree, to those forces—and only some of us choose a chemical solution.

So I can not adequately explain why I became an addict. I can, however, tell you *how* I became one: I used drugs until drugs used me. Until it hurt. And long afterward.

I used despite my religious upbringing, despite thousands of dollars of psychiatric therapy, and despite the care and concern of those around me. I was bright, but I kept on using. I was socially acceptable, but that just played into my denial. I kept quitting, but I couldn't stay quit. I tried so hard, so desperately hard, to recreate the "good old days," when drugs were, for me, such innocent, carefree fun—an exercise in futility that lapsed over into a kind of insanity that put me irrevocably over the line.

I started with pot in 1971, when I was seventeen, and it made me feel more comfortable with myself than anything in my life had up until that point. Along the way, I tried LSD (about a dozen times), mescaline, quaaludes, hashish, valium, and, to a much lesser degree, "ups" (speed) and "downs" (barbiturates). I never became much of a drinker, but I do recall getting drunk enough at parties to become sick and/or really hung over about once or twice a year during my late teens and early twenties.

Drugs were downright desirable then, even necessary. They were considered a potent tool for spiritual growth, social change, radical self-transcendence, and off-the-planet sex. They cemented social relationships, helped establish new ones more "spontaneously," and helped define my generation. At the time, I believed these things. I felt there was a profoundly spiritual aspect to getting high. You became more open to the idea of alternate realities and the interconnectedness of all things. Society was far too joyless and straitlaced—it *needed* some serious loosening up. Besides, how could anyone ever figure out what the lyrics to a Bob Dylan or Grateful Dead song meant *unless* they were high?

The important thing was to use drugs "responsibly," and, for a long time (about ten years), I was quite adept at maintaining some semblance of control. I kept up my grades. I got married, stayed steadily employed, and even started my own successful business. I was very "socially acceptable"—a weekend, intersession, and summer-vacation user. And then the weekends started to begin on Thursday night. And then came cocaine . . .

I vividly remember my first impression of the cocaine high: "This isn't spiritual at *all!*" I should have stayed with that line of thinking. It would have saved me so much grief. But, instead, in a fairly rapid fashion, the "spiritual" rationalization of my drug use fell by the wayside. I soon lost my desire for the other chemicals. Cocaine seemed to give me the confidence and energy I increasingly needed to stay atop my growing business and my ever more complex life—but that's just how it *seemed*. In reality, I was becoming addicted. And without knowing it. Addiction is the only disease that tells you you don't have it.

Without going into painful details, my life soon became unmanageable. I violated my own values and the trust of others. I became unreliable, dishonest, and highly preoccupied. I was using to live and living to use. The worst thing was that there seemed to be no end in sight.

And there wasn't, until I entered NA (Narcotics Anonymous). Although I attended mainly to appease my wife, I felt something at that first meeting that sparked some hope—enough to keep me coming back. Here were people with drug-abuse histories as long and sordid as mine (or worse!), who nevertheless were managing to stay clean for impressively long periods of time. Here was a place where you could say anything that was on your mind and people would nod in empathy. NA was shelter from the storm, a place where addicts didn't have to lead miserable, isolated, and dishonest lives. A place where "misfits" could finally fit.

Almost from the beginning, I sensed something wonderfully spiritual about these recovery meetings. For one thing, they were free; nobody was making any money off me. The idea of fellow and sister addicts getting together to help each other was very appealing—and *good* in every sense of that word. People in the program, when they weren't expressing some hurt, anger, pain, or dissatisfaction, appeared genuinely content. And, even when they were expressing pain, it seemed to be accompanied by faith and gratitude.

Most spiritual of all, however, were the Twelve Steps, the guidelines that have functioned as the framework for most of the thousands of self-help groups that now exist. Much has been written about the Twelve Steps elsewhere, and they have been a path to a healthier, happier life for millions of people who have suffered from a wide range of destructive habits or abuse by others, but the main thing to realize is that, regardless of one's particular affliction, the steps offer a *spiritual* approach to the problem. Not a religious one, but a spiritual one.

As a Jew, of course, it is more within my tradition to ask questions than to provide answers. Asking questions is important; it makes us think, it makes us search, it helps us grow. The first question that God asked Adam back in the Garden of Eden, "Where are you?," continues to hang in the air for all eternity. It is a question that echoes within every room of recovery and within every thirsty soul.

Those questions helped me, perhaps forced me, to look for connections between the recovery tradition and the Jewish tradition as I understood them. I found an abundance of such connections. My initial fears that recovery might be incompatible with my particular religious tradition were replaced with the understanding that nothing could be further from the truth. Even better: I found that my continuing growth in recovery was making me a better Jew, and that my Jewish knowledge and background was not harming but actually enriching my recovery. I was experiencing a kind of spiritual synergy, which led me to a feeling of serenity or *shalom*. To have it requires some wisdom and strength, some acceptance and some work, but these blessings are freely available to all who want them. The important thing is to begin . . . and to have faith. As Rabbi Nachman of Bratzlav said, "The entire world is a narrow bridge, but the main thing is not to fear." Let us cross that bridge together. If we but believe it, we are never alone.

AARON Z.

How To Use This Book

While this book provides the reader with its own unique blend of inspiration and affirmation, it is also a companion to the Torah: the spiritual touchstone of the Jewish people. As a result, its sections follow the traditional cycle of the weekly Torah reading. Just as the Torah is divided into weekly portions so that its entire contents might be read in public over the course of a year, so too is this book designed. However, the Hebrew (soli-lunar) calendar does not precisely follow the secular (solar) calendar. Different adjustments—through double portions—are made each year according to a traditional rabbinic formula.[1] You might want to simply read this book one day at a time, or one week at a time. In that case, begin at the beginning and keep on reading. However, if you choose to use this volume as part of your Torah study and wish to keep in sync with the Jewish world around you, consult the chart on p. 187–88. This will help you follow the traditional reading for any given calendar year.

Since Torah is read on Mondays and Thursdays, texts have been chosen directly from the Torah portion for these days. The Sunday section as well is introduced by a text from the Torah. Texts from other Jewish sources guide us through the middle of the week. Shabbat frames our week and offers us time for leisurely study. Thus, a Torah text on Friday is used to introduce Shabbat and an inspirational essay emanating directly from the text helps shape our thoughts for this special day.[2] In this volume, both authors' voices are heard during the weekly study of the Torah portion. On Sunday, Tuesday, Wednesday, Friday, and Shabbat, Rabbi Olitzky offers the reader spiritual insights from Jewish tradition. On Mondays and Thursdays, Aaron Z. offers a message from the depths of his experiences in recovery.

---

[1] Each year different portions are doubled in accordance with the holiday schedule, which is fixed by rabbinic formula. In order to approximate a secular year with fifty-two weeks, the portions Tazria and Metzora have been doubled (joined together) in this volume since they often are doubled in the yearly cycle of Torah readings.

[2] Please note that the last Torah portion, Vezot Ha'berachah, is not a regular Shabbat weekly portion. It is reserved for Simchat Torah, at which time the Torah is concluded, rolled back to the beginning and begun once again (with Bereishit). Therefore, the section for Vezot Ha'berachah follows a slightly different format from the rest of the book.

The Twelve Steps
of
Alcoholics Anonymous

The Twelve Steps are reprinted and adapted with permission of Alcoholics Anonymous World Services, Inc. Permission to reprint and adapt the Twelve Steps does not mean that AA is affiliated with the program. AA is a program of recovery from alcoholism—use of the Twelve Steps in connection with programs and activities which are patterned after AA but which address other problems does not imply otherwise.

1. We admitted we were powerless over alcohol—that our lives had become unmanageable.
2. Came to believe that a Power greater than ourselves could restore us to sanity.
3. Made a decision to turn our will and our lives over to the care of God as we understood Him.
4. Made a searching and fearless inventory of ourselves.
5. Admitted to God, to ourselves, and to another human being the exact nature of our wrongs.
6. Were entirely ready to have God remove all these defects of character.
7. Humbly asked Him to remove our shortcomings.
8. Made a list of all persons we had harmed, and became willing to make amends to them all.
9. Made direct amends to such people wherever possible, except when to do so would injure them or others.
10. Continued to take personal inventory and when we were wrong promptly admitted it.
11. Sought through prayer and meditation to improve our conscious contact with God as we understood Him, praying only for knowledge of His will for us and the power to carry that out.
12. Having had a spiritual awakening as a result of these Steps, we tried to carry this message to alcoholics, and to practice these principles in all our affairs.

(The use of the masculine pronoun in referring to God is the original AA language. Like many Twelve Step programs, we have chosen not to use a pronoun at all later in our discussion, but retain the original here.)

Renewal, like a livelihood, must be earned each day.

Genesis Rabbah 20:9

Personal Thoughts and Commitments
for
Self-Renewal This Week

Vayikra: Personal Sacrifices
Leviticus 1:1-5:26

**Whether one offers much or little
makes no difference, if only one's heart
is directed to God.**
Sifra to Leviticus 1:17

- ✔ The standard sacrifice is described, as an introduction to the sacrificial system which follows. This is a voluntary offering brought by an individual.

- ✔ In thanksgiving, the Israelites are instructed to offer the sacrifice of well-being, a festive meal eaten by the one bringing the sacrifice and his guests. Often this is referred to as a peace-offering.

- ✔ The sin-offering comes next, followed by a guilt-offering which is prescribed as a penalty.

Sunday

**He shall bring it to the entrance of the Tent of
Meeting, for acceptance on his behalf before Adonai.**
Leviticus 1:3

Here our souls are bared. There is no room for cleverness or deceit. Nor is there any need. In Tents of Meeting or rooms of Fellowship. Be open and honest. It's hard—but you are among friends. Really!

1

Monday

If one's offering is a burnt-offering of the herd, one should offer a male without blemish . . .
Leviticus 1:3

Of the freewill offering described in Leviticus 1:3, Rashi comments: "They press him until he says 'I wish to do it.'" What kind of a "freewill" offering is that? The answer of Maimonides is that the concept of "pressing" cannot be applied to performing the Divine will. *We really want to do good,* he teaches, but our evil urges press us in the opposite direction. To be pressed away from our evil inclination, according to this reasoning, is not a matter of duress, since bad behavior, in our heart of hearts, is really not our choice. With similar but more succinct wisdom, a Yiddish proverb tells us, "No choice is also a choice."

Every day, the most important choices addicts make are whether or not to get high, to eat more, to take a chance with the perfect system at the track, to look for love with just one more person. The choice is as clear-cut as life and death, but our disease is such that it is not always an easy one to make. We have thoughts, we have urges, we have people, places, and things that remind us of how it was . . . and we also have built-in "forgetters" that make our memories of active addiction focused more on the highs and less on the lows.

The fact is that the choice to use is always there. We are all always close to that next sexual conquest or box of chocolates. Recovery is never a given. It may very well be essential to our well-being, but that doesn't make it an obligation. Misery is always an option. Sometimes, when our disease tricks us into feeling uncomfortably deprived, restricted, or "pressed," it may help to change our perspective: Instead of saying "no" to drugs, say "yes" to recovery. The choice is ours.

Tuesday

**When wood burns it is the smoke alone that rises upward,
leaving the grosser elements below. So it is with prayer.
The sincere intention alone ascends to heaven.**

Baal Shem Tov

And so it is with recovery. We can leave the garbage behind us if
we really want to be healed. And if we don't—well, you know, it
continues to tempt us wherever we go, whatever we do.

Wednesday

**All the enthusiasm that spiritually awakened people have
when trying to do good is very precious, even if their goal
is not achieved. All their effort is counted like a sacrifice.**

Rabbi Nachman of Bratzlav

So all you have to do is try. Take the first step toward repentance, renewal, and recovery by taking the first step. Then
keep walking forward.

Thursday

And one shall bring forth one's forfeit to Adonai for the sin which he committed . . . as a sin-offering.

Leviticus 5:6

"Offer the sacrifices of righteousness," the Psalmist tells us (4:6) and indeed has a point. Just as the sacrifices specifically prescribed in this section of the Torah are necessary to atone for various misdeeds, so are sacrifices required for us to remain good—sacrifices not of animals, not of money, but of ourselves. To reach any goal requires not only focus and determination, but also the foregoing of a part of ourselves. As the saying goes, we can have anything we want, we just can't have *everything* we want.

In our quick-fix society, it is often too easy to do things that are illegal, immoral, or fattening. Instant gratification is the spiritual opposite of sacrifice. But the results are usually as fleeting as that twenty-minute (second?) high many of us so insanely pursued.

Just as athletes in training forego many of life's pleasures to achieve their goals, so we in recovery can learn to put doing what we need to do ahead of doing what we want to do. Making meetings and honoring service commitments may sometimes interfere with our living a "normal life," but, then again, so did using.

The bottom line is that recovery is work. Doing the right thing may not always be easy, but it is always the right thing. Now that we are no longer "burnt out," we have so much more to offer.

Friday

And he shall be forgiven.

Leviticus 4:31

Relief. A wholesome feeling. Just know that when you bring your sacrifice of self, you will be forgiven. But you have to bring it. Otherwise, there is nothing there to forgive.

Shabbat

Or when a person touches an unclean thing.
Leviticus 5:2

There is no in-between in addiction or in recovery. Once you touch it, you are back to where you were. Just once is too much. So don't touch it. Just as Shabbat is a sacred time which reminds us to stay away from things and activities that are secular, the recovery process reminds us to stay away from everything and *everyone* who will bring us down. Shabbat is a heavenly experience, a heightened state of awareness. In it, we transcend the dirt of our world, and for twenty-four hours we are elsewhere. Unlike an artificially induced journey, Shabbat is real, and even when we say goodbye to it on Saturday evening, we carry its memory with us throughout the week. Sabbath moments, we call them. And as a result, Shabbat carries us.

There is a recovery saying that "Halfhearted measures will avail us not." The magic in Shabbat is that it does not really work unless we are willing to make a serious and consistent commitment to "make Shabbat," not just when we feel like it.

Recovery is work, but it is also about giving ourselves a break. By making a clear, clean break—a separation—between the days which are ordinary and the day which is extraordinary, we strengthen our ability to let go and let God . . . in.

Questions for Self-Reflection

1. What am I prepared to sacrifice in order to continue in my recovery?

2. How shall I express my thanks to God for this newfound sense of well-being?

3. If I have sinned, what can I do to resolve the guilt that I feel?

Notes to Myself

Sacred Thoughts for Holy Living

Once Rabbi Yochanan ben Zakkai went forth from Jerusalem. Rabbi Joshua accompanied him. They beheld the Temple in ruins. "Woe is us!" cried Rabbi Joshua. "The place where Israel's sins found atonement is laid waste." But Rabbi Yochanan said, "Do not weep. We have means of atonement equal to this: deeds of love. As it is written, 'It is love I desire, not sacrifices'" (Hosea 6:6).

Avot de Rabbi Natan 4

For Renewal, A Psalm

I enter Your house with burnt offerings
I pay my vows to You
Those that my lips pronounced
That my mouth uttered in my distress.
I offer up fatlings to You, with the odor of
    burning rams,
I sacrifice, a bull and goats.
Come and hear, all those who fear God so
    that I can tell what You did for me.
I called aloud to You with glory on my
    tongue.
Had I an evil thought in my mind,
Adonai would not have listened.
But God did listen
You paid heed to my prayer.

Psalm 66:13-19

A Prayer

Adonai, I have sinned, I have transgressed. I have rebelled against You, I and my household. Adonai, pardon the sins, transgressions, and rebellions which I and my household have committed against You.

From the Confession of the High Priest,
Mishnah Yoma 3:8

Personal Thoughts and Commitments
for
Self-Renewal This Week

Tzav: Getting It Right
Leviticus 6:1-8:36

These are the rituals . . . with which Adonai charged Moses on Mount Sinai when God commanded that the Israelites present this offering to Adonai in the wilderness of Sinai.
Leviticus 7:37-38

✔ The offerings of the previous portion are reviewed a second time, but in more depth.

✔ The ordination offering is described and detailed, a sacrifice of well-being.

Sunday

The offering to Adonai . . . must be presented by the one who offers a sacrifice of well-being.
Leviticus 7:29

If you want to get your recovery right, you have to stay in touch—with yourself, your sponsor, and with God. Don't wait until the times get rough. Keep talking, and stay in touch.

Monday

This is the law of the burnt-offering, of the meal-offering, and of the sin-offering, and of the guilt-offering, and of the consecration-offering, and of the sacrifice of peace-offerings.

Leviticus 7:36

So many offerings and laws. But all are for the purpose of providing spiritually fresh starting points—for getting right and staying right. It's important to bear in mind that God's commandments are not necessarily ends in themselves. They may be pathways designed for our spiritual elevation. When our actions are in accordance with the Divine Will, as we understand it, we feel better. There is harmony, purpose, and greater spirituality.

This self-fulfilling aspect of the *mitzvot*—or the Twelve Steps—is worth keeping in mind, because addicts, moreso than most, have an intense aversion to being told what to do—even if it's for their own good. That, in a nutshell, is the insanity that lies at the heart of active addiction: We would rather continue our unhealthy but comfortably familiar patterns "our way" than ask for help.

In recovery, we learn how much better life can get if we don't follow our urges, although, quite often, that is easier said than done. In Judaism, there are hundreds of spiritual object lessons that can bring us closer to God—and they, too, can be demanding. Addicts . . . *people* . . . are generally better at indulgence than self-discipline. But self-discipline is generally a whole lot better for us.

Tuesday

**God made humans straight, but they have sought
a multitude of inventions [to stray].**

Ecclesiastes 7:29

Nobody has to list them for you. You know them all too
well—all the things you did to stray from the path that God
set before you. We are all like newborn babes . . . when we
return. Pure potential. You make the choice.

Wednesday

**A person without self-control is like a city
stormed and its walls shattered.**

Proverbs 25:28

We can't get recovery right without self-control. It's the key.
Without control, there is no self.

Thursday

**And the fire upon the altar shall be kept burning
thereby, it shall not go out.**

Leviticus 6:5

The Jerusalem Talmud comments, "It shall not go out, even
when it travels" (Yoma 4:6). Good advice for recovering people! Some of us enter recovery with "the gift of desperation."
We live, drink, eat, and sleep recovery, as if our lives depend-
ed on it, as indeed they do.

And then comes a tendency to get complacent, to coast. But,
as Dr. Abraham Twerski has observed, "If you're coasting in
neutral, you're probably going downhill." As long as I am in
my regular routine, my recovery works fairly well. But times
when I am away traveling (or when my wife and kids are
away), my disease senses a golden relapse opportunity. "No
one will know," it tells me. "You'll be able to get away with
it . . . ." Except that I would know. And I have learned how
terribly difficult it is to stop, even after "just once."

Getting recovery right means all the time and in every place.
Our ancestors carried the fire with them through their forty-
year journey in the wilderness. We need to carry the desire to
recover within us, too, wherever we go. And, if the fire is
burning too low, guess where you can go?

Friday

**He shall then . . . carry the ashes outside the
camp to a clean place.**

Leviticus 6:4

As in sacrifices, there is always something to clean up in recovery. Don't let it stay there and pollute the renewed life you have
built. Take it to a clean place. Better, take it to a place that
needs cleaning. There is always more work to be done.

Shabbat

If one offers it for thanksgiving.
Leviticus 7:12

When the messianic era is upon us, there may be no need for sacrifices, say the Rabbis. But the offering of thanksgiving will never cease. Although all prayers may be discontinued, the prayer of thanksgiving will never cease. Rather, the Jerusalem Talmud reminds us, "A new prayer shall be said every day" (Berachot 4:3). Recovery helps us to recognize things for which we should be thankful. These may not have occurred when we were immersed in the depths of our addiction. Recovery sharpens our senses. It makes us more responsive to the lush wonder of the universe. We are over-awed by God's creation. We are indeed thankful. For the first time in a long time, we feel alive. Such everyday feelings are worthy of prayer.

A friend, early in her recovery, told us that she was not sure whether or not she believed in God and was trying to reconcile that doubt with her sponsor's suggestion that she simply try praying to her Higher Power. When she walked at night and beheld the vastness of the evening heavens and the twinkling of the far-away stars, she had a profound sense of something greater than herself. She said the following: "I don't know if you exist, God, but if You do, thanks for helping me stay clean today." Learning how to be thankful is an important step in our spiritual growth.

But our prayer is not one that is just uttered from the lips, not one in which the sacred text of our people is mouthed, not even one which is carefully constructed out of our contemporary experience. Instead, our prayer is expressed in the way we live our lives, the acts of goodness we perceive and pursue.

Questions for Self-Reflection

1. Do I really have to do things the exact same way each time?

2. How do I express my sense of obligation in regard to living a Jewish life?

3. Is God always present when I make my own sacrifices in an effort to getting things right once again in life?

Notes to Myself

Sacred Thoughts for Holy Living

According to the Babylonian Talmud (Yoma 87a), when one makes a confession in order to repent, the phrase, "I shall sin and repent" must be repeated twice. Rabbi Huna had learned from Rav that when one has committed a transgression once or twice, it appears to him as if he is now permitted to do it. Each time the transgression is easier, and he eventually forgets that it is wrong. Thus, the individual is instructed to say "I shall sin and repent, sin and repent."

For Renewal, A Psalm

I will sing of faithfulness and justice;
I will chant a hymn to You, Adonai.
I will study the way of the blameless; when
    shall I attain it?
I will live without blame within my house.
I will not set before my eyes anything base;
I hate crooked dealing;
I will have none of it.
Perverse thoughts will be far from me;
I will know nothing of evil.

Psalm 101:1-4

A Prayer

O Eternal One, many are tired and lonely; teach us to be their friends. When those in denial are on their way to destruction, give us strength to "let go and let God." When the alcoholic/addict reaches out for help, give us the words of wisdom that will guide them to us. When confusion leads to anxiety and uncertainty, help us to calm their fears. When evil darkens our world, give us light. When despair numbs our souls, give us hope. When we stumble we fall, give us faith. When we lose our way, be our guide. Through You, may we find serenity, peace and understanding.

*From the JACS Shabbat
morning service*

Personal Thoughts and Commitments
for
Self-Renewal This Week

Shemini: In the Sanctuary

Leviticus 9:1-11:47

A person should have no other purpose in whatever is done, be it great or small, than to be drawn to God like iron to a magnet.

Moshe Chaim Luzatto

- ✔ The ordination ceremony of the priest takes place.
- ✔ Nadab and Abihu, sons of Aaron, are consumed by a "strange fire," following an unauthorized offering.

Sunday

Drink no wine or other intoxicant, you or your sons with you when you enter the Tent of Meeting or you will die. It is a law for all time throughout the ages.

Leviticus 10:1

Nothing really new. You knew it all the time. But now we all know it and have said it out loud. If you drink and drug, you will push God's protective sanctuary away from you, and you will die. There is no other—or better—way to say it.

Monday

And Nadab and Abihu, the sons of Aaron . . . offered strange fire before Adonai, which had not been commanded.
And there came forth fire from before Adonai, and devoured them, and they died before Adonai.

Leviticus 9:23

Although they had good intentions, the Rabbis comment, Aaron's sons took the law into their own hands with this spontaneous (and, according to Rashi, wine-inspired) and illicit modification of the holy sanctuary service. They neglected to ask Moses or Aaron for advice. Another commentator says that the two men were not actually drunk but approached their sacred task with perception and rapture not of Divine origin. Self-inspired as opposed to God-inspired. Taking too much liberty . . .

Their death by an equally unusual fire, as described in the Midrash, uncannily parallels the dire fate of many a cocaine user. According to the Midrash, this Divine fire split into four fiery threads, entering each of the priests' nostrils. It killed them from the inside, leaving their bodies and garments untouched. Strange fire, indeed.

Too often, even in recovery, we think we have all the answers when experience has painfully indicated otherwise. Today, we can avoid the spiritual pitfall of such arrogance by asking for the help we need.

Tuesday

Menachem Mendl of Premislan once wrote that there are three things fitting for us to do: upright kneeling, motionless dancing, and silent screaming.

Not everyone will understand your pain or your path to recovery. That path requires a special kind of behavior, the kind that takes us into God's sanctuary.

Wednesday

The consumption of abominable things causes a deterioration of the soul so that it descends from a human to a beastly level.

Moshe Chaim Luzatto

It's a pretty strong statement, but you know what Luzatto is talking about. Do the drugs, take the drink, eat too much or too little, keep on gambling, go from bed to bed and what *do you* become?

Thursday

And Moses made diligent inquiry concerning the goat of the sin-offering . . .
Leviticus 10:16

One commentator, Rabbi Aaron Lewin, bluntly states that this constitutes half the Torah—not the specific law itself, but the attitude of high regard for the law, so that even a Torah maven, one who knows it all, like Moses, would carefully deliberate a law's fine points before taking any action.

The Sanctuary and the sacrificial system are both spiritual safeguards designed to bring the Israelites closer to God and to atonement, to reinforce their faith, and to prevent their feeling hopelessly lost in the wilderness.

Twelve Step programs also exist to protect us from ourselves, to promote healthy thinking, and to keep us from feeling lost, lonely, and disconnected. For us, "diligent inquiry" means "thinking it through." What will happen if we act upon an urge to use? How will it feel afterward? Could we stop at "just once?" Did we ever? Could we come back to a meeting and admit our slip? Or would it more likely be that we would not *want* to come back? And what then?

We have a way of acting impulsively on issues that might better be dispassionately considered—and for procrastinating on others that would benefit from immediate action. Today, let us pray for the wisdom to know the difference.

Friday

They brought to the front of the Tent of Meeting the things that Moses had commanded and the whole community came forward and stood before Adonai.
Leviticus 9:5

Even in a community, supported by those who truly care about us, we must face God as individuals. Each is responsible for what he or she does. Our burden is shared by others, and that makes it lighter, but it's still an individual burden.

Shabbat

For you must distinguish between the sacred and the profane, between the unclean and the clean.

Leviticus 10:10

This is the work of a lifetime. Not only do we have to recognize the difference between the sacred and the profane—and sometimes that's not easy—but once we realize which is which, we have to keep the profane away from us. At the same time, we have to work hard to make the sacred a part of our lives.

If you're using and abusing, don't even try. You won't be able to get it right, and so it gets you wrong. The Rabbis tried it by turning Purim into a *simcha shel mitzvah,* the happiness derived from the performance of a mitzvah, expressing that joy through wine. We know better. Of course you'll mix up Mordecai and Haman if you're drunk. This is not something you want to get mixed up in. You've participated in this Purim-sanctioned topsy-turvy on so many non-Purim days that you've earned a lifetime exemption.

Rebbe Moshe of Uheli once dreamed that he was being led into Paradise. Yet all he saw was a group of sages studying Torah. There was nothing remarkable. The rebbe was disappointed. In his life he had expected Heaven to be far more exotic. Suddenly a man called out to him: "Moshe, son of Hanna. Do you really think that the sages are in Heaven? You have it wrong. It is Heaven that is in the sages."

Questions for Self-Reflection

1. Have I been silent in God's midst when I should have spoken up?

2. What more can I do to make room for a sanctuary in my life?

3. Have I honestly considered how I have profaned my life with booze and drugs, compulsive sex, eating, or gambling?

Notes to Myself

Sacred Thoughts for Holy Living

The Sabbath itself is a sanctuary which we build, a sanctuary in time.

Abraham Joshua Heschel

For Renewal, A Psalm

Fortunate are those who dwell in Your house.

May they continue to praise You.

Fortunate is the one whose strength is in You.

Upstanding ways are in their heart.

Psalm 84:5-6

A Prayer

At dawn, I seek You, my Rock and Refuge

I offer my morning prayers and those in the evening.

Contrite, I tremble in Your awesome Presence.

For You pierce even my innermost thoughts.

What can my tongue or even my heart do?

Of what use is the strength of my spirit in me?

Only to be mortal music, sung sweetly to You

As long as I live, will Your praises sing within me.

Solomon ibn Gabirol

Personal Thoughts and Commitments
for
Self-Renewal This Week

Tazria/Metzora: Personal Defilement and Ritual Purity

Leviticus 12:1-13:59/14:1-15:33

**A person cannot make atonement
with what he did in sin.**
Babylonian Talmud, Temura 20b

✔ One can ritually defile oneself through various means, which are listed: childbirth; *tzaraat*, a kind of skin ailment usually translated as leprosy, which can penetrate a house and garments; discharges from sexual organs.

✔ Instructions for ritual purification are also included.

Sunday

He shall call out, "Unclean; unclean."
Leviticus 13:45

The first time we hear it, we cringe with pain—but it's true. We know it. What should be the response? Yes, we're unclean. But help us to get clean and stay clean.

Monday

**When a person shall have in the skin of his flesh
a rising, or a scab or a bright spot . . . then that
person shall be brought to Aaron the priest or to
one of his sons the priest.**

Leviticus 13:2

Have you ever wondered why other people can offer such
brilliant insights into your own behavior? It's really not sur-
prising. They simply don't have as much energy and attention
tied up in defending your ego as you do. They can, in short,
be more objective. It is probably in this sense that the
Mishnah states, "Persons see any plague except those on oneself" (Negaim 2:4).

Tzaraat, the biblical disease mentioned extensively in this
week's portion (and one generally translated as "leprosy,"
although some commentators disagree), was said to be caused
by arrogance. Only the priests could diagnose it. And the
treatment was indeed quite humbling: The afflicted person
could not enter the Sanctuary, was regarded (until cured) as
dead, and was quarantined.

The disease of addiction also made us social lepers. Even if
we were "socially acceptable," we didn't feel that way inside.
Besides, in the arrogance of active addiction, we weren't
ready to listen. We were too busy pedaling furiously on that
vicious cycle.

Even in recovery, it remains easier to solve someone else's
problems than our own. And, certainly, one should be ready
to listen and help, if asked. But it's a good idea to keep the
focus on yourself. Recognizing your own spiritual blemish is
not the same thing as beating yourself up over your imperfections. It may be the first step in cleaning them up.

Tuesday

**Personal cleanliness is the foundation of
spiritual purity; it is the path by which one
reaches the Heavenly realm.**
Babylonian Talmud, Avodah Zarah 20b

You can't feel clean until you are clean. If you rid yourself of
the dust on the outside, there will be no place for the dust on
the inside to hide. Just wash it clean and stand a little taller.
Then take a step toward Heaven. You'll get there. Just keep
on walking.

Wednesday

If you sanctify yourself a little, you are sanctified.
Babylonian Talmud, Yoma 39a

Just get started. God picks up the slack. Process makes perfect
—or at least as close as we'll ever get.

Thursday

**As for the living bird, he shall take it and the
cedar-wood, scarlet, and hyssop, and shall dip
them and the living bird in the blood of the bird
that was killed over the running water.**

Leviticus 14:6

This is the purification ceremony pertaining to lepers on the
day of their cleansing. It is replete with symbolic significance.
One bird is killed, and one bird is set free, but not before
being dipped in the blood-and-fresh-water of its unluckier fellow captive. The essential message of this, as well as of all
other ancient sacrificial rituals, couldn't be clearer: Something
dies, so that something else may live. There, but for the will of
God, go I.

So powerful was this communal need in ancient times, that
Judaism was radically ahead of its time in prohibiting human
sacrifice. Nevertheless, the gore and primitivism of it all may
be distasteful to the modern reader, myself included.

We perhaps have evolved shrewder and more ecstatic forms
of self-defilement and sacrifice, but one fact remains relent-
lessly blunt from then until now: Some of us make it, and
some of us don't. People die from alcoholism and drug addiction and eating disorders. People suffer from compulsive
gambling and sex. Not everyone makes it into the rooms of
recovery meetings. Not everyone stays. We have found a better way, thank God, but remember those who didn't. Thank
them during your next moment of silence. In this way, they
did not die in vain.

Friday

He shall wash his clothes and he shall be clean.

Leviticus 13:6

It *is* possible to transcend your past, to let go of all of that
unnecessary baggage that weighs you down. Let it go and be
done with it. When you are clean, nothing can make you dirty.

Shabbat

You shall put the Israelites on guard against their uncleanness, lest they die through uncleanness by defiling My Tabernacle which is among them.
Leviticus 15:31

Staying clean is hard, but it was harder to get clean in the first place. And that was not so long ago. No need to jog your memory. You remember it as if it were yesterday. And when you don't remember, someone in your community will be there to help you remember. If we cannot remember our past, we are doomed to repeat it. Don't forget: Not only will chemical substances defile you, but they also will eventually destroy you. In the meantime, they will defile those around you by destroying your relationships with them. It's like playing dominoes, and everyone loses.

Now be on your guard. Don't make excuses for yourself or anyone else. When you see abuse in your community, don't keep it a secret. Confront it. Let the world know. Addiction is impossible unless someone starts using. No one can use or abuse without your consent. You have a choice. Think about it, and then do something about it.

Staying clean is not just a message for the addict or abuser. It's for everyone. All of our lives are dirty in one way or another. Get rid of the dirt, and get out of the wilderness. It's holy work, but someone has to do it. Recovery is learning to be partners in our own creation, the creation of a better self.

Questions for Self-Reflection

1. When will I finally feel clean?
2. Have I honestly faced the uncleanliness of my ways?
3. What should I do to purify my body and my soul?

Notes to Myself

Sacred Thoughts for Holy Living

Repentance waits patiently at all times for human beings. When can a person be purified of iniquity? When that person returns to the Ruler on High and utters a prayer from the depths of one's heart.

Zohar III, 69b

For Renewal, A Psalm

Your fury lies heavy with me.

You afflict me with all Your breakers. Selah.

You force my companions to shun me.

You make me abhorrent to them.

I am shut in and cannot go out.

My eyes pine from my affliction.

I call to you, Adonai, every day

I stretch out my hand to You.

Psalm 88:8-10

A Prayer

Grant me a generous spirit, humility and modesty, a good portion in life, and good companions. Our God and God of our ancestors, may Your name not be profaned through me. May I not become a mockery or a curse among fellow creatures. May I be assured of a future. May my hope not be snuffed out by despair. Grant me a share in Your Torah, with all who do Your will. Save me from all harsh decrees. Do not turn me away unanswered. Answer my prayers.

Adapted from the prayerbook
of Amram Gaon

Personal Thoughts and Commitments
for
Self-Renewal This Week

Acharei Mot: Arrogance and Atonement

Leviticus 16:1-18:30

For on this day atonement shall be made for you to cleanse you of all of your sins; you shall be clean before Adonai.

Leviticus 16:30

✔ The preparation to enter the Shrine is discussed at length, now that Nadab and Abihu—who were inadequately prepared—are dead.

✔ The provisions for Yom Kippur as a model for atonement are described in detail.

✔ More laws about sacrifices and food are given.

✔ There is an introduction to the biblical view on sexual morality.

Sunday

You shall not copy the practices of the land of Egypt.

Leviticus 18:3

For the Rabbis, Egypt is the symbol of all of our enslavements, including the temptations of the flesh. To be a Jew is to be wholly different. Keep telling yourself that just because others are doing it doesn't mean that you have to do it as well.

Monday

And he shall make atonement for the Holy Place . . . and so he shall do for the Tent of Meeting that dwells with them in the midst of their uncleanness.

Leviticus 16:16

The Baal Shem Tov said that this verse implies that arrogance is the worst sin, because it explicitly states that, even when the Israelites were defiled with sin, the Holy Presence never left them. The only exception to this Divine "blanket coverage" was the sin of arrogance. As the Talmud states: "God said, 'There's no room in the world for both the arrogant and me'" (Sota 5a).

Elsewhere in this week's portion, we are told that those who do not bring the atonement sacrifice shall be "cut off" from their people (Leviticus 17:9). Active substance-abusers often are so far gone into their artificial realm, that they no longer participate in family or community activities. Even when they are present in body, they are not all there. Their disease wants them to be somewhere else. The sense of shame and sneakiness that every addict has felt is profoundly alienating, to say the least.

Perhaps this is why the Rabbi of Lublin said that he preferred a wicked person who knows he is wicked to a righteous person who knows he is righteous. The wicked person still has some truth in his heart that connects him with God, but the righteous person who considers himself righteous is not righteous at all, but arrogant—and thus cut off from God.

We can never improve if we think that we are beyond reproach. We can never let God or other helpers in if we are so smugly self-contained. God does not expect us to be perfect—just better. And the willingness to be better is very much at the heart of both recovery and atonement.

Tuesday

**It is impossible to be joyful unless one is humble.
The arrogant are insatiable and can therefore
never experience true joy.**
Rabbi Nachman of Bratzlav

If you continue to be arrogant, recovery will elude you. And
there will be no place for atonement in your life. Anyhow, if
you're so great, why are you here in the first place?

Wednesday

**When Moses received the Torah, regarding sacrifices he
asked, "Master of the universe, what shall the people of
Israel do when they are in exile?" God replied: "Let them
study the Torah. It will serve them as an atonement more
effectively than all their sacrifices."**
Midrash Ha'neekun I, 100a

Submerge your arrogance in the pages of Torah. All preten-
sion and presumption will be lost. You'll see. The more you
learn, the more you realize you don't know. And you'll want
to study more. That's the joy of Torah study and its reward.

Thursday

And Aaron shall lay both his hands upon the head of the live goat, and confess over him all the iniquities of Israel, and all their transgressions, even all their sins; and he shall put them upon the head of the goat and shall send him away . . . into the wilderness.

Leviticus 16:21

If you didn't know that this is where the idea of a scapegoat comes from, today you can be grateful for learning something new.

Many of us effectively became the scapegoats of our families. We were the ones with the glaring problems. But scapegoats don't happen by themselves. As the Jewish people have unfortunately discovered throughout history, we very often are just a label to conveniently assign blame. Ironic, isn't it, that the original purpose of the biblical scapegoat was to promote forgiveness?

It is easy and tempting and human nature to blame and to point fingers, but it doesn't change anything except for the worse. Festering anger and regret is a slow-acting poison for the soul. Recovery shifts the focus from blame to forgiveness: forgiveness from God, forgiveness for others, and forgiveness for ourselves. We may have a whole bunch of reasons, explanations, and excuses for why we became who we are—but that won't necessarily help us change for the better. The important thing is that today, in recovery, we don't have to be anybody's scapegoat anymore.

Friday

Do not defile yourselves . . .
Leviticus 18:24

The Torah text couldn't be much more explicit. You are a sacred vessel of mind, body, and soul. Keep the junk out of you and away from you. Atonement is more than just saying, "I'm sorry." Many rabbis have said it, but Simcha Bunam said it best: "You can tell that the sin you committed has been pardoned by the fact that you no longer commit the sin."

Shabbat

**It is a sabbath of complete rest for you, and you shall
practice self-denial: it is a law for all time.**
Leviticus 16:31

Yom Kippur is the model, and recovery is the method. It's not
one day in time, it's one day at a time.

We start with ourselves. It's the only place to start. And we
look at our lives—where we went astray, what we did wrong.
Then we take a deep breath, gather what little strength is left
and go about fixing what we broke. And the cost of repair
gives us renewed strength. It's not an easy task. It's hard work.
Don't let anyone mislead you. But the results are phenomenal.
We begin to feel alive once again, actually sensing the blood
coursing through our veins. We begin to heal. And as we heal,
one of the broken vessels in the world, the pieces of our shattered life, is made whole once again. We will never forget our
past. It will serve us as a reminder of where addiction can lead
us. As we continue to heal, God continues to forgive.

Having learned to forgive ourselves, let us learn to forgive
others. It's the next step in the process. Holding fast to
grudges and past resentments hurts no one more than ourselves. Others have wronged us, just as surely as we have
wronged others, but there comes a time to escape that infernal
loop. Let today's complete rest give us a sense of completion
about our past. Those battles are over; lay down your weary
anger. We are strong enough today to forgive others and to
pursue peace in ourselves.

Questions for Self-Reflection

1. What else must I do to humble myself so that I can fully atone for my past?

2. How can I carry the message of Yom Kippur to the rest of my year?

3. Who should I approach for forgiveness if I have scapegoated instead of accepting responsibility for my own actions?

Notes to Myself

Sacred Thoughts for Holy Living

No one's prayer is given hearing unless when he raises his hands in prayer, he also raises his whole soul heavenward in his hands.

Babylonian Talmud, Taanit 8a

For Renewal, A Psalm

Let those who seek my life
Be frustrated and put to shame;
Let those who plan to harm me fall back in disgrace.
May those who rejoice at my misfortune be frustrated and
   utterly disgraced;
May those who vaunt themselves over me be clad in
   frustration and shame.
May those who desire my vindication sing forth joyously;
May they always say, "Extolled be Adonai
Who desires the well-being of Your servant,"
While my tongue shall recite Your beneficent acts,
Your praises all day long.

Psalm 35:26-28

A Prayer

I confess to You, who are perfect, all my flaws and imperfections. You know them even better than I, but You want me to acknowledge them freely. I confess my hypocrisy and smugness, my lack of feeling and double standards. They are not easy to see. Help me to see them.

I confess to You, because You are patient, the times I have been vain or obstinate. Give me common sense. Let me see myself as others see me, and be content.

I confess to You, who understand me, all my small and silly deeds. With embarrassment I remember my pettiness, my white lies, my lack of tact, and half-truths. Help me not to mislead others or be tripped up by them.

From the prayerbook of the Reform Synagogues of Great Britain,
Forms of Prayer for Jewish Worship

Personal Thoughts and Commitments
for
Self-Renewal This Week

Kedoshim: A Life of Holiness
Leviticus 19:1-20:27

The whole purpose of *mitzvot* is to elevate humankind.

Leviticus Rabbah 13:3

✔ The biblical prescription for a life of holiness is described.

✔ Holiness begins with sanctifying the reputation of God and by not profaning it by sinful acts.

Sunday

Do not curse the deaf, and before the blind do not set an obstacle, and you should fear your God, I am God.

Leviticus 19:14

Jewish commentators explain the reference to the blind as inclusive of anyone who is unaware, "blind to the fact." It thus becomes a transgression to trick people. This passage is most interesting, because it instructs us to be responsible to our conscience. How fine a dictate this is when preparing to make amends to all those we have harmed, even those who never realized that they were conned. Equally as remarkable is that this is offered as a path to achieve holiness.

Dr. Benzion Twerski

Monday

You shall be holy, for I, Adonai, your God, am holy.
Leviticus 19:2

Maimonides said, "When the Bible says, 'Be holy,' it means exactly the same as if it said, 'Do My commandments.'" The Kotzker Rebbe said, "Be holy—but be a *mensch* (that is, a decent, compassionate, down-to-earth good guy or gal with integrity)." In Judaism, the two are not exclusive.

A student once was studying Torah so fervently that she could not hear her baby crying. Her rabbi, observing this, told her, "You are not studying Torah properly if you are oblivious to your child's needs." Holiness is rituals and study, yes—but it is also being nice and doing for others. Helping a neighbor, giving to charity, visiting the sick are every bit as holy as meditating on a mountaintop.

Everyone comes into the program to deal with his or her "problem," but he or she stays for the spiritual growth. If all you want to do is give up your addiction or avoid your compulsive behavior, but you're not willing to change, you'll be miserably abstinent—and that's not what recovery is about.

The first few steps clear up the confusion and restore our faith; the middle steps are atonement, reconciling us with our past; and the final steps clearly point towards a heightened spirituality. Holiness is eating, breathing, thinking, and living God's will to the best of our ability and understanding. It's the kosher way of getting higher.

Tuesday

Self-respect is the fruit of discipline. The sense of dignity grows with the ability to say no to oneself.

Abraham Joshua Heschel

That's how we begin to turn our lives around. When we respect ourselves, we won't want to invite our destruction. And we start with a single two-letter word, No!

Wednesday

I dwell on high in holiness yet with the contrite and the lowly in spirit.

Isaiah 57:15

When we speak of God, we usually think of distant heavens way beyond our reach or even conception. Heaven is not a place. It is a space, one we enter when we are connected to God, who lives there.

Thursday

**. . . and you shall love your neighbor as yourself:
I am Adonai.**
Leviticus 19:18

Rabbi Akiba said that this is the fundamental principle of the Torah. It is interesting that this injunction against resentments, grudge-bearing, and selfishness concerns one's relations with fellow human beings and not with God. The essential message of the Torah—be considerate of others—is itself a powerful example of God's compassion. I see the phrase, "I am Adonai" as the other side of the spiritual equation: "If you can be so un-self-centered as to love your neighbor as yourself, it is tantamount to acknowledging that I am God."

Of course, if we don't love ourselves, if we are filled with hatred, plagued by fear, or tormented by insecurity, our ability to love is impaired. We are too busy nursing our wounds or trying to fill our emptiness to give a damn about anyone else. *The noise in our heads can sometimes deafen our hearts.*

One of the great things about recovery is how it restores self-respect along with compassion and respect for others. As the group accepts us, we learn to accept ourselves. By being honest and sober, we have much less of which to be ashamed. Our behavior becomes more harmonious with our values. We learn that helping others, sometimes just by listening, makes us feel good about ourselves.

Helping others as we help ourselves is the spiritual essence of every Twelve Step fellowship. We are fortunate to have the opportunity to practice Leviticus 19:18 every time we go to a meeting. And guess what? It works.

Friday

Reprove your neighbor but do not incur guilt because of him.
Leviticus 19:17

Sometimes being nice is not the right thing to do. Social conventions generally do not save lives. If your friend is using or abusing, don't make up excuses. Help her, but don't get caught in her web of self-deception. Let your life of holiness be large enough to envelop her as well.

Shabbat

The stranger who resides with you shall be to you as one of your citizens, you shall love him as yourself, for you were strangers in the land of Egypt.
Leviticus 19:34

The challenge of today is to stop being a stranger to yourself. If we feel like a stranger to ourselves, it is only a matter of time before we start to act strangely. Perhaps you don't even know who you are anymore. Would the you that you once thought you were do the things you used to do? Included in this biblical edict may be the suggestion to love the stranger within us: the dark, furtive part that makes us feel guilty, ashamed, and thoroughly unlovable. When you make that stranger your friend, he's not a stranger anymore. And when you become your own friend, you don't have a desire to be someone else. Then you stop looking for things to do and drugs to take that will turn you into that someone else, because you can never really be someone else. Essentially, you are who you are. What you make of yourself is up to you.

"Only as the soul knows itself can it know its Creator," says our sage, Abraham ibn Ezra. Get to know yourself better. Examine yourself in the mirror of your life. And then bask in the light of that knowledge, in the Light of all knowledge.

Questions for Self-Reflection

1. What can I do to realign my life to make it holy?

2. Does my life sanctify or profane the name and reputation of God?

3. What can I do to repair the sacred relationship I have broken or betrayed?

Notes to Myself

Sacred Thoughts for Holy Living

Let an individual be aware against going forth on his journey alone. That is to say, let him obey the Divine will so that he shall not go forth without the accompanying presence of God—which will sustain him and deliver him in every hour of need.

Zohar I, 459

For Renewal, A Psalm

I cry aloud to God;

I cry to God that God give ear to me.

In my time of distress I turn to Adonai
   with my hand [uplifted];

I cry all night without respite;

I will not be comforted.

I call God to mind, I moan,

I complain, my spirit fails.

Then I recall the deeds of Adonai.

O God, Your ways are holiness.

Psalm 77:2-4, 12, 14

A Prayer

Eternal Source of good, we thank You for the gifts and blessings that fill our clean and sober days; for life itself, and its endless twists and turns; for all that sustains body and mind; and for the excellence of Your Torah, which deepens our life and enriches our days.

From the Shabbat evening service of JACS

Personal Thoughts and Commitments
for
Self-Renewal This Week

Emor: Responsibility

Leviticus 21:1-24:23

When a person is occupied with the needs of the community, that person is occupied with Torah.

Jerusalem Talmud, Berachot 5:1

✔ The laws concerning the priests and their role in society are listed. From these role models, behaviors for the common folk are derived.

✔ The festival calendar and the appointed festivals of Adonai are fixed.

✔ More rules for the Temple cult: the oil for the lamp stand, the shewbread, and what to do about the blasphemer.

Sunday

You shall not profane the place sacred to me.
Leviticus 21:23

Imagine if the world were filled with signs saying, "This is God's place. Don't use; don't abuse." Well, the signs are there. You just haven't learned yet how to read.

Monday

They [the priests] shall be holy unto their God, and not profane the name of their God; for the offerings of Adonai made by fire, the bread of their God, they do offer; therefore they shall be holy.

Leviticus 21:6

Earlier chapters of Leviticus regulate how the community should stay clean by proscribing certain behaviors and instituting a system of penitential sacrifices. But since the priests are so intimately associated with God's Dwelling Place, special laws are accorded to them. A higher standard.

Twelve Step meetings do not happen spontaneously. And while the program's traditions forbid leaders, we do have such "trusted servants" as chairpeople, secretaries, treasurers, and coffeemakers who have accepted the responsibilities that these positions require on behalf of the group.

In the parlance of the rooms, these positions are called "commitment," and, as group wisdom puts it, "Commitments keep you clean." For by accepting a commitment, you are indicating your willingness to do more: more for your group and more for your recovery. Responsible spiritual leadership is not about ego gratification or dominance. It is about setting more of yourself aside to serve the needs of the community.

Tuesday

Preoccupation with watching other people's blemishes would prevent me from investigating my own, a task more urgent.

Joseph ibn Pakuda

Take responsibility. It's easy to blame others for who we are, but no more. We are no longer what we did. Instead, we are what we have become.

Wednesday

Retreat is the beginning of defeat.

Babylonian Talmud, Sota 44b

Don't turn back now. You've come too far. You have faced the task and made it your own. *Kadimah* now, onward.

Thursday

And you shall not profane My holy name; but I will be hallowed among the children of Israel.

Leviticus 22:32

What we say and what we do matters, in the Jewish view, not only because God wants us to act a certain way, but also because our behavior can influence others. Our behavior can attract others toward God or away from God. Do we practice what we preach? Or are we talking just to talk.

The very *idea* of God is sacred in Judaism—not something to be taken lightly or defiled in word, thought, or deed. Any religious person, Jewish or not, takes upon himself or herself the additional responsibility of being a kind of "ambassador of God's will." Her life, in effect, testifies not only to her beliefs and values, but also to personal worthiness and admirability.

Rest assured, none have nor ever will fulfill that responsibility perfectly, but it's worth keeping in mind, and it is applicable to recovery not because of what they have or how they look, but because of who they are. They're friendly, happy, self-assured. They give of themselves without making a big deal about it. And they are particularly sensitive to reaching out to the newcomer, who is very much a stranger in a strange land.

There's a lot of laughter and jocularity at meetings, but at the expense of ourselves, not of recovery. Recovery can and should be as joyous as possible, but never something to be taken lightly. To do so is to leave the door wide open towards profaning ourselves.

Friday

Anyone who blasphemes God shall bear his guilt.

Leviticus 24:15

It is difficult to be rid of guilt. Perhaps we never really *should* be completely free of it, especially if it keeps us acting responsibly. We sinned. A lot. And we are responsible for what we did. Don't let the guilt drag you down. Let it be an impetus to raise you up.

Shabbat

The first day shall be to you a sacred occasion.
Leviticus 23:2

While Friday evening and Saturday comes every week regardless of whether you acknowledge them or not—simply as a measurement of time—you have to take responsibility for Shabbat to arrive; you have to welcome it into your home and into your life. As you begin your recovery, you begin to take responsibility for your life as well, for who you are and what you have become. Frequently such responsibility is overwhelming. It's paralyzing. The experience of Shabbat provides you with the foundation of spiritual strength which you need to assume that responsibility, more and more each week. From Shabbat take all that you need. It is an endless reservoir. But don't just stop there. Use it as an anchor for your entire week. Some people measure time in relationship to the experience of Shabbat. Some start it early; others prolong it by waiting until as late as Wednesday to make *havdalah*. And that's OK, because Shabbat is only a couple of days away. Let Shabbat become your metaphor for recovery—calm and serene, peaceful and protective. With enough faith and footwork, our entire life can become more filled with sacred occasions, whatever the day, by turning off the stopwatch in our lives. Each Shabbat is a glorious way to stay. Take responsibility for your recovery and for living a holy life.

Questions for Self-Reflection

1. What models of my behavior need to be refined?

2. How can I anchor my life in the fixed calendar of the Jewish people?

3. What is my responsibility to myself? And to my people?

Notes to Myself

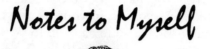

Sacred Thoughts for Holy Living

A person in a boat began to bore a hole under his seat. When fellow passengers asked him what he was doing, he answered: "What do you care? Am I not boring under my own seat?"

Leviticus Rabbah 4:6

For Renewal, A Psalm

Oh how I love Your face.

It is my meditation all day.

Your *mitzvot* make me wiser than my enemies.

For they are always with me.

I have retrained my feet from every evil way

In order that I might observe Your word.

Psalm 119: 97-98, 101

A Prayer

Master, O Divine friend to Your serene house.

We may have strayed from the right path.

But we paid the price in every kind of pain.

You, Adonai, are our defense and hope.

Each day we wait for Your Divine grace

To redeem us and to make us like an abundantly
   watered garden.

From a "Berach Dodi" hymn by
Rabbi Simeon ben Isaac of Mayence

Personal Thoughts and Commitments
for
Self-Renewal This Week

Behar: Redemption

Leviticus 25:1-26:2

Redemption, like a livelihood, must be earned each day.
Genesis Rabbah 20:9

✔ The Sabbatical, during the seventh year, when all land has to be fallow and all debts are remitted, is described. The close of seven sabbatical cycles constitutes the Jubilee when all debtors and slaves are set free.

✔ The Israelites are given instructions regarding the treatment and eventual release of slaves.

✔ A unique perspective on blessing and curses is offered.

Sunday

The more such years, the higher price you pay.
Leviticus 25:16

The more you work the land, the more it will take to reinvigorate it. The more you abuse your body, the more it will take to cleanse it, the longer the time to jubilee.

Monday

**. . . in the Day of Atonement shall you
make proclamation with the horn
throughout all your land.**
Leviticus 25:9

The Day of Atonement and the Jubilee have much in common besides the shofar blast. Just as slaves were freed on the Jubilee, so does the Day of Atonement free us from the enslavement of bad habits, bad behavior, and guilt. That the two are so closely linked in the Torah is no coincidence. As Hillel said, "If I am not for me, who will be for me? And if I am only for myself, what am I?"

Our fate—as alcoholics, as addicts, and as human beings—is a common one. In the Jewish view, what we do or don't do affects not only us, but also the spiritual well-being of the world.

So Hillel's famous comment can be amended as follows: If I don't work to free myself, who will work to free me? But if all I do is flaunt my own freedom, without regard to the needs of anyone else, then what am I but a slave to my own ego? When it comes to recovery, freedom, and love, we can't keep what we have unless we are willing to give some of it away.

Atonement, recovery, ancient sacrifices, the Jubilee: All are means of liberating ourselves from past mistakes and situations, and of getting back in touch with that part of us that wants to be good, joyous, and free. That forever pure part of us . . . our soul.

Tuesday

Redemption is like the dawn.
Pesikta Zotarti

Imagine a cold desert night, and you are sleeping on the ground. The temperature continues to drop, and you get colder and colder with each passing moment. After a long night, the sun awakens the world, gently caressing you with sunshine. That's the warmth of redemption and recovery.

Wednesday

**Do not say, "Tomorrow we will be redeemed."
We may miss the moment now.**
Menachem Mendl Ussishkin

Tomorrow is a long way off. It never really gets here. For redemption to come, we have to work for it now. If we wait for tomorrow too long, it quickly becomes yesterday. Redeem yourself now. Get straight. Get sober. Stay away from the poker table.

Thursday

And you shall hallow the fiftieth year, and proclaim liberty throughout the land.
Leviticus 25:10

Every fiftieth year, the Torah instructs, slaves are to be freed and property is to revert to its original owners. Thus an economic leveling of the playing field takes place, a biblical "restructuring." But, aside from its being Divinely decreed, wherein lies the holiness of the Jubilee year?

The answer is twofold. On the one hand, it is a massive act of national charity. The Torah only works if we are free to pursue it. Poverty and slavery can deaden the soul as effectively as compulsive sex. Anything we can do to liberate a fellow human being is a holy act, and the Torah mandates this once-in-a-lifetime liberation opportunity.

But the even deeper holiness implicit in this law may be that it acknowledges who the real owner of land and souls is. None of us own. We are all here on borrowed time, and our possessions are but gifts. In the comfort and complacency of material wealth, we may prefer to forget that, but the Jubilee ensures that we don't.

Recovery may be a once-in-a-lifetime opportunity for redemption, too. I often have heard addicts confess doubt about whether they "have another recovery left in them." That is a healthy doubt. Every relapse opens a door to active addiction that is very hard to close. Don't assume that you'll be able to come back easily, or at all. Jubilees do not happen every day.

Friday

Do not wrong one another.
Leviticus 25:17

When you provide excuses for others, enabling them to continue their addiction, you are wronging them. Help them to get straight and keep straight.

Shabbat

You shall not make idols for yourselves.
Leviticus 26:1

How easy it is to make idols out of our addiction. Even in recovery, we too often replace our substance of choice with something else: from alcohol to cigarettes, from sex to food. These addictions are less benign, perhaps, but they still steal our lives away. There is only one God deserving of our attention. The Twelve Steps, however spiritual, are not religion. At best, they provide a neutral model, one which we fill out by the faith that we bring to it, by the community in which we share it. Anything that is made into an idol in our lives is potentially dangerous. Steer clear of it. The Israelites were confronted by idols wherever they turned. They even tried to make one themselves. It didn't last long, but it could have destroyed the Jewish people. We bear the burden of that legacy, know how it feels.

In his *Sefer Ha'aggadah*, Chaim Nachman Bialik relates the following parable: A king who was angry with his son began to beat him harshly. One of the king's friends who was present looked on but was afraid to intercede. However, as soon as he heard the king say to his son, "If our friend were not sitting here, I would kill you!" the man immediately took action. "The matter now rests with me," he said. He intervened and saved the boy.

The opportunities for redemption are ever present. Just look for them. If you do, they will find you.

Questions for Self-Reflection

1. What things do I still feel enslaved to and need release from?

2. What resource of mine have I overworked that now needs to lie fallow?

3. How can I change my perspective to see a blessing in the midst of what I previously perceived as a curse?

Notes to Myself

Sacred Thoughts for Holy Living

When human beings languish in pain, let no one say, "I shall return to my own household, eat and drink and be at peace." No, each person must be willing to suffer with his neighbor. The one who shares the afflictions of others will next behold the comforting of humanity.

Babylonian Talmud, Taanit 11a

For Renewal, A Psalm

It is good to chant hymns to God

It is pleasant to sing songs of glory.

Adonai rebuilds Jerusalem

You gather in the exiles of Israel.

You heal their broken hearts

And bind up their wounds.

Psalm 147:103

A Prayer

I confess to you, my truest friend, my need for friendship. There are times when I have felt let down, and even betrayed. Help me to remember the times which I have not kept faith with others or let them down. Then perhaps my failures may join me to them through understanding, even if I cannot love.

I confess to You, the power of love, the times I have felt unloved, or been unable to love enough. In the coming year give me the power to love, to give without price, and receive without excuse.

I confess to You, for in You I trust, the desires of my heart which make me ashamed, and the suspicions in my mind which are neither right nor justified. I should like the courage to face them, accept them as my own, and with Your help transform them.

From the prayerbook of the Reform Synagogues of Great Britain,
Forms of Prayer for Jewish Worship

Personal Thoughts and Commitments
for
Self-Renewal This Week

Bechukotai: Blessings and Curses
Leviticus 26:3-27:34

I will establish My abode in your midst . . . [but] if you do not obey Me . . . I will wreak misery on you.
Leviticus 26:6, 14-16

✔ The Torah teaches us the function and extremes of *tochechah* (rebuke).

✔ What is yet due to the sanctuary—vows, gifts, and dues—is explicitly outlined.

Sunday

Those of you who survive will be masters over their iniquity.
Leviticus 26:39

If you survive, you will have learned the lesson of addiction well and be able to share it with others. But only if you survive. Learn from what others have taught us. Stay away from things that will do you harm. God has given us a choice: blessing or curse, life or death. Choose life—so that we may all live.

Monday

. . . you shall eat your bread until you're satisfied.

Leviticus 26:5

As the Book of Proverbs says, "The righteous eats to the satisfying of his desire, but the belly of the wicked shall want" (13:25). What is addiction but a perpetually insatiable craving? We try to fill a spiritual emptiness with chemicals or food or sex, and it brings temporary relief at first and then not even that.

Recovery brings us back to basics and to the simple joys of life. And eating warm bread is one of the best! By becoming more content with who we are, we become more easily and naturally satisfied. We're off the treadmill, living one day at a time. We eat when we're hungry and sleep when we're tired.

Following God's will for us helps keep us balanced and whole-hearted. Where there was fear, now there is faith. Where there was self-obsession, now there is self-esteem and humility. We don't have all the answers—and *we don't need to*. Someone else is in control.

It's ironic that the very drugs and drinks we thought would stimulate our senses eventually just deadened them and we lost our appetite for everything else. Today, whether it's a tasty meal, a hug, or a walk outside, we can be grateful for being able to enjoy once again the blessed little pleasures of life.

Tuesday

**I will establish a new covenant with you,
written on the very hearts of the people.**
Jeremiah 31:31

That's the best place to write it. Any place else we might forget. But there, where we feel the most love and the most pain, the blessing and the curse, there these will be remembered and understood.

Wednesday

A curse has no abode where a blessing was pronounced.
Tanhuma 58

The only way to keep clear of a curse is by shutting it out of the room with blessings. Blessings are deeds, not words. Say it, then do it!

Thursday

**And I will break the pride of your power and I will make
your heaven as iron and your earth as brass.**

Leviticus 26:19

The hidden blessing of hitting bottom is that it is suddenly,
painfully, and irrevocably clear that "our way" is seriously
flawed. It is that acute insight that leads us to seek help.

To believe that we are our own Higher Power is not only the
utmost of arrogance but also one of the most insidious, ego-
intoxicating, and prevalent forms of insanity. For the person
who believes it, the world becomes a barren, unyielding
place. And when we become so spiritually oblivious that we
no longer even have the inclination to stop and smell the
roses, then we might as well be made out of plastic—or brass.

Thus, to read these verses of the Torah as so many Divine
"carrot-and-stick" promises and threats is to miss their
metaphorical meaning. Just as doing God's will is its own
reward, so is walking contrary to God its own punishment. It
estranges us from God in heaven, from our fellow human
beings on earth, and most of all, from ourselves.

As the Baal Shem Tov said, "There is no room for God in the
person who is full of self." Some of us had to reach a point of
hellish hopelessness to realize this, but the blessing of recovery is that we don't have to live that kind of cursed existence
again. We have found that following God's will is a healthier
way to live.

Friday

If a person consecrates his home to Adonai . . .

Leviticus 27:14

Our homes are our sanctuaries—not because we say so, but,
rather, because we make them so. Let God's presence fill your
home by providing a place of sanctuary for those you love,
those who need your help. Don't shut them out. Welcome
them home—clean.

Shabbat

If you do not obey Me . . . I will wreak misery on you.
Leviticus 26:14-16

Rebuke. Tough love. That's the only way to recovery. Everything else is second-rate and will never work. You can count on that. God knows our nature better than we do. God knows that in order to get Israel to return, God will not be able to mince words. No excuses. No apologies. No ambiguity. Our souls are on the line. It's either Torah or tragedy. The choice really is that clear. It is only our stiff-necked egos that obscure it. Without Torah, we cannot really live.

When you want to help someone to get clean and stay clean, you also must do it without excuses or apologies. But God is saying something else as well: If you do not live a life of Torah, you will bring disaster on yourself—and on everyone around you. God won't have to do anything. You'll mess everything up all on your own. And the walls will keep tumbling down.

Now's your chance to change all of that. No more rebuke is necessary. You've seen the curse. You've lived it. Now's the time to live the blessing. It's hard work. But someone has to do it.

Questions for Self-Reflection

1. How can I express my love to others without "enabling" them (unintentionally fostering their addiction)?

2. If I am chastened now, what vow should I make to keep my life on track?

3. Now that I have been blessed, what can I do to extend that blessing to others?

Notes to Myself

Sacred Thoughts for Holy Living

Two students came to the Magid of Mezeritch and asked how it is possible to fulfill the Talmudic obligation to praise God for misfortunes with the same joy as when one praises God for good fortune (Berachot 54a). The Magid advised them to ask Rabbi Zusya who lived in extreme poverty, with only a dirt floor and barely the necessities of life as well as painful physical ailments. The students went to Rabbi Zusya and found him studying Torah. They put the question to him, but Zusya was puzzled. "I don't understand why the Magid sent you to me," he said. "I have never experienced anything bad in my life. Only good things have happened to me."

For Renewal, A Psalm

O Jerusalem, glorify Adonai, Praise your God, O Zion!
For You made the bars of your gates strong, and blessed
    your children within you.
You endow your realm with well-being, and it satisfies
    you with choice wheat.
You send forth Your word to the earth;
Your command runs swiftly.
You lay down snow like fleece, scatter frost like ashes.
You toss down hail like crumbs—who can endure Your
    icy cold?
You issue a command—it melts them; You breathe—the
    waters flow.
You issue Your commands to Jacob, Your statutes and
    rules to Israel.
You did not do so for any other nation; of such rules
    they knew nothing.
Hallelujah.

Psalm 147:12-20

A Prayer

My God, You have given me over to starvation and poverty. Into the depths of darkness You have plunged me. You have taught me Your power and Your strength. But even if they burn me with fire, I will love You all the more and rejoice in You.

Medieval prayer, quoted by Bachya ibn Pakuda

Personal Thoughts and Commitments
for
Self-Renewal This Week

Bemidbar: In the Wilderness

Numbers 1:1-4:20

Where people truly wish to go, there their feet will manage to take them.

Babylonian Talmud, Sukkah 53a

✔ A census of the Israelites is taken.

✔ The Levites are separated and placed in charge of the Tabernacle with specific responsibility to the sons of Aaron.

Sunday

The Israelites shall stand guard around the Tabernacle of the Pact.

Leviticus 1:53

When you are in the wilderness, you have to be even more careful about the world around you. Temptations will not disappear. They simply will not interest you. But don't be fooled by your newfound strength. Stand your guard.

Monday

And Adonai spoke to Moses in the wilderness of Sinai . . .
Numbers 1:1

In between slavery and the promised land lies the wilderness. It is a transitional place, a no-man's-land where old habits can be discarded and new patterns of living can take root, unencumbered by any preexisting boundaries or expectations. In short, the wilderness is the perfect Torah training ground, where the children of Israel can focus on their spiritual development without the diversions of material or military pursuits. It is an anonymous place that is really no place at all, but rather a process.

When we enter a recovery program, it can feel like a wilderness. We are confused, beaten, and lost—sad-eyed strangers in a strange land with uncomfortable new rules. But that's only the way it feels. In truth, it was our active addiction that more closely resembled a desolate wasteland. Recovery, like the biblical wilderness, is actually a far more healthy and hospitable place than the slavery we left behind. It, too, will be a lifelong journey, but that's OK, so long as we are moving in the right direction.

Running insanely in circles gets us nowhere. This is a better way to walk: slowly and serenely. The joy is in the journey. We can feel good about the progress we've made. We have already come a long, long way.

Tuesday

**One goes forth and does not know where—
if for good or evil.**

Tosefta

When you set out on your journey, where you go is up to you. Feeling like you are back in the wilderness is part of the process, but remember: Not only is that where our ancestors wandered, it is also where they received the Torah.

Wednesday

**There is a way which seems straight to an
individual but its end is a path to death.**

Proverbs 14:12

The Israelites assume that the shortest route from Egypt to Canaan is the best one. But it is the long journey in the wilderness that changes slaves into free people ready to control their own destiny.

Thursday

. . . as they encamp so shall they set forward, every person in his place, by their standards.
Numbers 2:17

This section of the Torah clearly delineates the camp arrangements and marching sequence of the twelve tribes, imposing a logistical order upon the wilderness. Without order and discipline, no large assembly of people can long survive.

It is the nature of individuals to fall into patterns—some good, some bad. The lifestyle of the active addict may appear to be chaotic (and it is!); but even in it we can find a guiding, organizing principle.

Many of us resent routine and discipline, because it smacks of someone telling us what to do. The important thing to realize about self-discipline is that it is something we tell ourselves—and something that will benefit us. Anything really worth doing requires effort and organization. Just think of how important organization is to recovery: We attend meetings regularly, meetings that could not happen if they weren't scheduled for a specific time and place, and which have a set format.

Getting our lives back in order often begins with our mastering the simple, necessary activities of daily living that we had become sloppy about. Those people in the program who choose not to believe in God sometimes use that name as an acronym for Good, Orderly Direction. One of the many blessings of recovery is how it enables us to develop healthy new patterns in our lives.

Friday

Associated with you shall be a person from each tribe.
Numbers 1:4

As we have already learned, we can't journey alone. Fellowship, friends, and sponsors are there to help us find our way out of the wilderness.

Shabbat

Any outsider who encroached was to be put to death.
Numbers 3:38

Sometimes we have to hear the ugly truth—even when it hurts. The world is not perfect, nor close to it. Even in goodness, there is the potential for evil and pain. What we do with the raw material of life is up to us. But we don't have to tell *you* that. You know it. Any addict knows it. Anybody knows it. But living a clean life is one way of keeping the world's imperfections far from us. It also makes sure that we don't add to them. The further away you are from creating a sanctuary for yourself, the closer you are to a spiritual death. So live. Stay away from everything in this world that will drag you down. There is no need to test yourself. Holy living means that you should be wholly clean. Begin by staying away from alcohol and drugs, but remember that being drug free is only a beginning. If you don't stay away from the things that got you to that state in the first place, they will lead you there once again. The further down you get, the longer distance you have to climb back up.

In the Bible, direct access to the Sanctuary is limited to priests and their assistants. In the modern world, the sanctuary of Shabbat is only off-limits to those who would not make it their own, who do not come to it with clean hands and a pure heart, who do not come to it clean.

Questions for Self-Reflection

1. What kind of accounting of my household need I take?

2. How have I made my responsibilities sacred tasks?

3. How can I find my way out of the wilderness?

Notes to Myself

Sacred Thoughts for Holy Living

Have I not instructed you? Be strong and of good courage. Be not affrighted. Neither shall you be dismayed. For Adonai your God is with you wherever you go.

Joshua 1:9

For Renewal, A Psalm

Praise Adonai for You are good,

Your steadfast love is eternal.

So let those redeemed by Adonai say,

Those You redeemed from adversity.

Whom You gathered in from the lands

From east and west

From the north and from the sea.

Some lost their way in the wilderness,

In the wasteland

They found no settled place.

Hungry and thirsty

Their spirit failed.

In their adversity they cried to Adonai

And You rescued them from their troubles.

Psalm 107:1-6

A Prayer

Dear God, I beg you. Judge me with mercy. If you judge me in anger, you will annihilate me. Turn to me in mercy and bring me back to You in complete repentance. Be with my speech and with my thoughts. Keep me from sinning with my tongue. Think of me with love and mercy. Lead me in good ways because of Your greatness.

From Solomon ibn Gabirol, "The Crown of Glory"

Personal Thoughts and Commitments
for
Self-Renewal This Week

Naso: Ordinary Lives, Ordinary People

Numbers 4:21-7:89

Sinners are mirrors. When we see faults in them, we must realize that they only reflect the evil in us.

Baal Shem Tov

✔ A set of laws is related together, because each refers to persons to be excluded from the camp. They are ritually unclean.

✔ The events discussed are ordinary things which happen to ordinary people.

✔ The ordeal of Sotah water is outlined.

✔ This section includes the vows of the Nazirites and the priestly benediction.

✔ The portion concludes with the priestly offerings brought to dedicate the Tabernacle.

Sunday

Each one was given responsibility for his service.
Numbers 4:49

The routine life. Nothing special. That's the toughest thing to realize, that life is mostly routine. But we each have our own gift: what we do to contribute to life and the world around us. Something simple. Something special.

Monday

**This is the service of the families of the
Gershonites, in serving and in bearing burdens:
They shall bear the curtains of the tabernacle, and
the tent of meeting, its covering . . .**

Numbers 4:24-25

The original Tabernacle roadies! It is important to realize that
the Torah is not just about Moses and Aaron and Abraham
and Jacob, but about the entire Jewish nation. Perhaps that is
the spiritual meaning behind the census commanded by God:
that every person counts. We can't all be superstars, but we
can all be *mensches* and *menschettes*. We all have our special
purpose in life, and we don't even know what it is, but the
important thing is that we do it. And how can we do something if we don't even know what it is we are supposed to
do? By doing the best we can. By being the best person we
can be. Beyond that, "God will provide."

We live in a society that is obsessed with fame. Even recovery
has acquired a certain trendy status, as celebrity after celebrity tells his or her story in books and on the TV talk shows.
But, from a spiritual viewpoint, there is no such thing as the
ordinary. Every moment, every life has the potential for
goodness, and goodness is better than greatness. Making it
through the day without using a drink or drug may not seem
like a heroic achievement, but for an addict, on certain days,
it most certainly is.

To live a quiet, decent life full of compassion and good deeds
will not get us on the six o'clock news, but it will help us
recover. Thinking that we're "less than" or not good enough
is one of the many ways our disease lies to us. As we grow
spiritually, we learn to better appreciate how extraordinary
the ordinary can be.

Tuesday

Rabbi Hillel said that one ought to teach every individual, for there were many sinners in Israel who were drawn to the study of Torah and from them descended good, pious, and worthy folk.

Avot de Rabbi Natan 3

Each and every one of us has an imperfect legacy. Ordinary people, ordinary families, with ordinary backgrounds. No kings and queens. Only a holy nation that stood at the foot of Sinai and beheld God's presence. Pretty ordinary!

Wednesday

There is not one good person on earth who does what is best and does not err.

Ecclesiastes 7:20

We are all just plain folk. Even the best among us does not lead a perfect life. Live the best you can. Before you criticize your neighbor, remember that she's living the best she can. Life is tough. We are bound to make mistakes. That's what being human is all about.

Thursday

When a man or woman shall commit any sin that people commit . . . then they shall confess their sin . . . and make restitution.

Numbers 5:6-7

It is hard to live with a guilty conscience and impossible to recover with one. No less than seven of the Twelve Steps deal with examining our wrongdoing and shortcomings, confessing them to God, ourselves, and another human being, making amends, and continuing to monitor ourselves.

Both the Torah and the steps recognize that even with the best of intentions, people are not perfect. Sooner or later, we're going to make a mistake. These mistakes can be quite "ordinary"—a lie here, an unkind word about someone there, treating someone unfairly, dishonesty with ourself through rationalization or denial—but their adverse effect can be profound. We feel guilty, uncomfortable, spiritually fragmented. And sins have a way of leading to more sins.

Admitting we're wrong, making amends, and resolving to improve our behavior is not always easy—but neither is living in pain. Doing teshuvah restores our spiritual cleanliness, removes the soul-crushing burdens of guilt and infallibility, and gives us a fresh start. Just as recovery does. And we don't have to wait until Yom Kippur or when we're working through the steps to reap the benefits of atoning, either. Anytime we're ready to stop feeling bad about something we've done is a good time to do something about it.

Friday

The priest shall bring her forward and have her stand before Adonai.

Numbers 5:16

It is not possible to sin against someone else and not sin against God, as well. As sinners, we all stand before God with our guilt. And as a people of God, we are all forgiven.

Shabbat

**If anyone, man or woman, explicitly utters a
Nazirite vow to set himself apart from Adonai . . .**
Numbers 6:2

In recovery, we are ordinary people, only more so. Perhaps that's what it was like to be a Nazirite. Ordinary, but more so. For the special vows of a Nazirite are rather ordinary, especially for us. No drink, no drugs. We make that vow every day. We are consecrated to God. It is a special relationship—available to anyone, anytime. Holy lives are for holy people. Let our lives become an example for living for everyone, especially those around us. Let our vows of abstinence, which we repeat daily, remind us of the commitment we have made to living, to life. And let us keep saying these vows aloud, to ourselves, in public, in private—whatever it takes to keep us clean. This is the life God intended us to lead, so that our heads would be filled with Torah and our hands could do holy work.

The Nazirite is not content with what is expected of the ordinary individual. The Nazirite needs to create a special life through special vows. The Nazirite often takes the vow in response to a miraculous event, as a form of giving thanks. The addict needs to do the same. But, unlike the addict's vow, the Nazirite vow is often temporary, beginning with thirty days and increasing from there. Begin your Nazirite vow with time periods that work for you—one hour, one day, one week, one month—but know that you will keep counting. Your vow is the vow of a lifetime.

Questions for Self-Reflection

1. What have I done that has excluded me from my community?

2. How have I broken sacred trusts with those I love?

3. What vow have I made to distinguish myself from other people?

Notes to Myself

Sacred Thoughts for Holy Living

The Baal Shem Tov once said, "The world is full of wonders and miracles, but human beings take their little hands and cover their eyes and see nothing."

For Renewal, A Psalm

Deal kindly with Your servant

So that I may live to keep Your word.

Open my eyes that I may perceive

The wonders of Your teaching

I am only a sojourner in the land,

Do not hide Your commandments from me.

Your decrees are my delight,

My intimate companions.

Psalm 119:17-19, 24

A Prayer

Adonai our God, treat us with compassion all the days of our lives. Assuage our fears, establish the work of our hands, heal our wounds, and save us from the grip of our enemies. May weeping and wailing not be heard in our homes; may destruction and devastation not be found within our borders. May we be worthy and reverent before You. Teach us Your Torah, and enlighten us in Your presence. Unite our hearts to revere You that we may prosper in all our paths, wherever we turn, until the day when You gather us unto You. Bring us from peace to peace that we may find tranquillity in our way of life in Your presence and delight at Your right hand forever.

From the prayerbook of Saadiah Gaon

Personal Thoughts and Commitments
for
Self-Renewal This Week

Behaalotecha: Leadership

Numbers 8:1-12:16

People see in their dreams only that which is suggested by their own thoughts.

Babylonian Talmud, Berachot 55a

- ✔ For those who were prevented from observing Passover at its proper time, a Second Passover is celebrated.
- ✔ The cloud signifying God's presence is again described.
- ✔ Silver trumpets are sounded for special occasions.
- ✔ As a result of the growing tension among the people, Moses realizes that he needs help.
- ✔ Moses shares his leadership with Joshua.

Sunday

Please do not leave us . . . be our guide.
Numbers 10:31

Even Moses needed help from others. To be a leader is to understand your strengths and your weaknesses, and to understand those of others.

Monday

**I am not able to bear all this people myself
alone, because it is too heavy for me.**
Numbers 11:14

When Moses feels that he no longer can bear the burden of leadership, he asks God for help, and God asks him to pick seventy elders to assist him. One of the main pitfalls of leadership is falling prey to the notion that you have to do it all yourself, that you are less of a leader if you ask for help. But a leader unaware of his or her limitations is an accident waiting to happen.

It is a shortcoming we all share. We tried to mask our vulnerability and terrifying sense of inferiority by pretending that everything was fine. Maybe we thought that was what we had to do in order to be socially acceptable, that if anybody ever found out how imperfect we really were, they'd lose us in a second. Or maybe we felt so isolated and unlovable that we seriously doubted that anyone would ever lift a finger to help us.

But the twin burdens of omniscience and omnipotence became unbearably hard. Maybe hitting bottom was God's way of helping us find *ourselves* out. Admitting that we have a problem that we could not solve by ourselves was the first time in a long time that many of us asked for help . . . and it continues to be the basis upon which our recovery works. We keep coming back to meetings in tacit acknowledgment of the fact that we still have a lot to learn from and benefit by them. Today, we can be grateful for having a more realistic sense of our limitations—and for being more able to ask for help.

Tuesday

You must pattern yourself to be like God. Just as God is merciful and compassionate, so you must be merciful and compassionate.
Babylonian Talmud, Shabbat 133b

Leadership is more than being at the front of the line. It means leading a life that others will want to follow. Don't just talk about the good life. Lead it.

Wednesday

Leadership shortens life.
Babylonian Talmud, Berachot 55a

We don't have to control everything. It's OK to let go. Not everyone can be a leader—nor wants to be. Just be yourself. Someone else can be a leader. Your turn will come—when it should.

Thursday

And Moses said unto him: Are you jealous for my sake?
Would that all of Adonai's people were prophets, that
Adonai would put the Divine spirit upon them.
Numbers 11:29

One of the signs of healthy leadership is not being threatened by someone else's talents. If I'm really confident about who I am, then I can accept you as you are. And, if I am a compassionate leader, then I welcome and encourage your growth: I want you to be as good as you can possibly be. It is a mark of spiritual maturity when we can stop comparing ourselves to others and truly admire their achievements.

Time and time again, the Torah reveals how Moses' leadership was not about self-aggrandizement but about selflessly serving the needs of the multitude. This is one leader who does not *need* to be a leader. A good thing, too, for the Talmud tells us that God weeps over a community leader who is domineering (Hagigah 5b).

The tradition of Twelve Step fellowships is that "our leaders are but trusted servants." The emphasis is on their responsibility to the group, not the group's allegiance to them. We have learned that the best way to lead is by example. Recovery cannot be imposed on anybody. We are more amenable to suggestions than to commands. Besides, learning to lead *ourselves* to a more sane and spiritual existence is challenge enough.

Friday

Moses was a humble man, more so than any
other man on earth.
Numbers 12:3

Moses did not seek leadership. He merely rose to it. Leadership takes various forms. Sometimes a leader is lost in the crowd and only rises to leadership when God calls out to him or her.

Shabbat

He drew upon the spirit that was on him.
Numbers 11:25

It takes a lot to be a leader. We have to draw on resources beyond ourselves. But, too often, we look for things that we think will make us more than who we are. Drugs, sexual conquests, gambling wins, food. These don't make us more than we are. They turn us into empty illusions of ourselves. Each of us has the potential to be a leader. In our own way, we are all leaders. Everything we do serves as an example for someone else. And the strength, the resolve for leadership is rooted in self, enhanced by the Divine spirit. So dig down deep. Draw on your own strength.

Maimonides compared the resting of spirit in this verse to the experience of one whose night is illuminated by flashes of lightning. In those brief flashes, we see all we need to see. And we keep the memory of what we have seen alive in our minds, so that it can illuminate the rest of the way. Maimonides went on to say that "for some it is given to behold the lightning flashes in rapid succession. They seem to be one perpetual light and then night is as clear as day."

Hillel put it a different way: "In a place where there is no human being *[mensch]*, strive to be one." It's especially important to do what is right when others have not done so. Rise to the responsibility. And do what is right, so that others may follow and do the same.

Questions for Self-Reflection

1. Can I muster the strength necessary to lead myself—and others—by my example?

2. Do I share my responsibilities with others?

3. Can I lighten my load and still be effective?

Notes to Myself

Sacred Thoughts for Holy Living

One of unblemished ancestry should not be put at the head of a congregation, for if a leader becomes too proud, it is good to be able to say, "Look back and see where you came from."

Babylonian Talmud, Yoma 22b

For Renewal, A Hymn

When the ark was set out, Moses would say,

Arise Adonai and scatter your enemies.

May Your foes flee from before You.

And when it halted, he would say,

Return Adonai, unto the ten thousand of the
    families of Israel.

Numbers 10:35-36

A Prayer

O God, I pray, heal her.
Moses' prayer on behalf of Miriam,
Numbers 12:13

Personal Thoughts and Commitments
for
Self-Renewal This Week

Shelach Lecha: New Terrain

Numbers 13:1-15:41

Without experience, there can be no wisdom.
Ben Sira 3:25

- ✔ As the Israelites approach the Promised Land, scouts are sent out. Only two among them return with a favorable report.
- ✔ The people murmur discontent. They are afraid to enter the new land.
- ✔ Miscellaneous laws about challah, Shabbat, strangers, and *tzitzit* are discussed.

Sunday

We came to the land you sent us to; it does indeed flow with milk and honey.
Numbers 13:27

Perspective. Some see new challenges and call them problems. Others call them opportunities and grow from them.

Monday

The Land . . . is a land that eats up its inhabitants; and all the people that we saw in it are men of great stature.

Numbers 13:32

The Hebrew literally translates "inhabitants" as "those who sit in it," to which the Rabbi of Ostrowicze commented that the Promised Land is a land in which one cannot sit still in one place (that is, one cannot stagnate spiritually there), but must move onward and upward at all times toward greater spiritual heights. Who, the spies, wondered, could possibly do this? To this, says the rabbi, Caleb replies, "We can indeed go up." Let us make ladders. We need not climb up to heaven all at once; it is OK if we do it by degrees—step by step.

The parallel to a recovery newcomer "spying out" a meeting is striking. Without faith, new situations always invoke fear. How much more so when we are trying to give up the one thing in our lives that has helped us combat our fears? The voice of our disease further fuels our fear: "Look at these people," it says, "clean and sober for months and years. *You'll* never be able to do that! And look how they're sharing their problems so honestly. You'll never be able to do that, either. You might as well just give up now and leave quietly, before they discover who you really are—a totally incurable mess!"

And yet, somehow, those of us who stayed made it. So we don't always have to listen to those voices of negativity within. The thing to remember about that committee inside your head is that all of its members are addicts, alcoholics, or co-dependents. Caleb has the right ideas: faith that God's will shall be done and a one-step-at-a-time approach to a challenging situation. When our disease tells us to F.E.A.R.—to Forget Everything And Run—we can be sure that we're just not looking at things the right way.

Tuesday

Neither a good dream nor a bad one is entirely fulfilled.

Adapted from Babylonian Talmud, Berachot 55a

Whenever you set out to do something new, you take a risk. Sometimes you succeed, and sometimes you fail. But you never really do all of what you set out to do. However, that little remaining piece propels you to do even more. Even *teshuvah,* a return to God and a renewal of spirit, is a journey that is never complete.

Wednesday

The light of a candle is useful when it leads you.
It is useless when it trails behind.

Bachya ben Asher, Kad Ha'kemach

When you set foot in new terrain, you need a lot of light. There's a lot of darkness, and you don't want to lose your way. So keep the light of Torah shining brightly in front of you. And you will be able to see where you are going.

Thursday

And all the Israelites murmured against Moses and Aaron, and they said, "Would that we had died in the land of Egypt—or would that we had died in this wilderness!"

Numbers 14:2

There's a saying around the Twelve Step program: "Be careful what you pray for—you might get it." The latter half of this characteristic congregational *kvetch* falls into this category. By readily accepting the pessimistic spy report and projecting onto the future the very worst outcome, the Israelites again demonstrate a deficit of faith and obliviousness to miracles. They are given what they ask for. Seemingly incapable of exercising the courage and conviction of a free nation, they must wander the wilderness for another thirty-eight years, until they die off and are replaced by a new generation free of slave attitudes.

New situations can cause apprehension in anyone—but for addicts and alcoholics, paralyzing terror is the norm! Our disease would convince us that the familiar misery of drugging and drinking is preferable to the dangers lurking behind closed doors. "We were in our own sight as grasshoppers," say the ten gloom-and-doom spies—and, yes, when our self-esteem is about one inch off the ground, that's about how tall we're going to feel. The bottom line, however, is that no one can make us feel inferior without our consent. Anytime we want to look at our very worst enemy, we simply can look in the mirror. But with restored faith and some gratitude today, we can better accept the uncertainties of tomorrow. It is, after all, only uncertain to us.

Friday

Why is Adonai taking us to that land to fall by the sword? Our wives and children will be carried off! It would be better for us to go back to Egypt.

Numbers 14:3

We all fear what is new and unknown. Even former addictions seem more comfortable. At least we knew that path. But face the challenge. Do not return to Egypt or even want to be there.

Shabbat

**When you enter the Land to which I am taking you
and you eat the bread of the Land,
you shall set aside a gift to Adonai.**
Numbers 15:18-19

When you attempt new things, when you enter a new phase of your life, know that everything is not going to go smoothly. This is important to keep in mind in our quick-fix culture where all of life's problems are quickly resolved on TV or in the movies, where miracle cure products are presented for whatever ails us. We don't just demand quick relief, we demand it to be effortless, too. We are led to expect the impossible out of life and are disappointed, if not outraged, when life refuses to cooperate with us. Life is hills and valleys. But mostly life is routine like flatlands. You will have successes and failures, achievements and setbacks. But it's all part of growing. Even as adults we grow. But we're more than adult children. We have to be willing to nurture our own growth. To do so we have to be clean and sober. No, you don't need the support of chemical substances or lots of food to brave a new job or a new relationship. Sex will not make him love you more. All you need is you—and those who love you.

Look at a new challenge as an opportunity for growth. Don't shy away from it. Embrace it. Make it your own. Consider it a gift from God. And be worthy of it.

The Israelites were afraid to enter Canaan, even though it had been promised to them by God. They did not know whether it would be a land flowing with milk and honey or totally uninhabitable. But that's really the way life is. We don't know what the future will be like until we live it. And that's OK. It's what makes life so interesting and the future so enticing—worth living for.

Questions of Self-Reflection

1. Do I fear new opportunities or consider them as challenges?

2. Am I critical of people and things just because I don't know them?

Notes to Myself

Sacred Thoughts for Holy Living

"When you call Me and come and pray to Me, I will hear you. When you seek Me, you will find Me. If you search for Me with all your heart, I will let you find Me," says Adonai.

Jeremiah 29:12-14

For Renewal, A Psalm

Give up anger, abandon fury,
Do not be vexed,
It can only do harm.
For evil-doers will be cut off;
But those who look to Adonai,
They shall inherit the land.
The lowly shall inherit the land
And delight in abundant well-being.

Psalm 37:8-9, 11

A Prayer

O merciful Creator, grant us the peace of Your holy Shabbat and help us improve our conscious content with You, as we pray to understand Your direction and the power to carry it out.

Adapted from the JACS
Friday evening service

Personal Thoughts and Commitments
for
Self-Renewal This Week

Korach: Rebellion

Numbers 16:1-18:32

**Do not fight against Adonai . . .
you will not succeed.**
2 Chronicles 13:12

- ✔ Moses faces the most serious rebellion of the forty years of wandering in the desert.
- ✔ The special duties of the priests, Levites, and Israelites are listed in response to Korach's rebellion, in order to protect the Sanctuary.

Sunday

**Truly it is against Adonai that you and your gang
have banded together. For who is Aaron that
you should rail against him?**
Numbers 16:11

There *are* times to rebel, to protest, to right the wrongs of an unjust world. But rebellion for its own sake, though it claims a righteous cause, is blasphemy.

Monday

And they assembled themselves together against Moses and Aaron, and said to them: "You take too much upon you . . . why, then, do you lift yourselves up above the assembly of Adonai?"
Numbers 16:3

One of the reasons why Korach is so effective at fomenting discontent is that he knows just what to say. The Midrash provides several examples of Torah texts that he would cleverly twist around to make them appear ridiculous. He knows—as do all demagogues—how to appeal to the "lowest common denominator." His basic message is, "You've been short-shrifted, you deserve more, you deserve to be more, just leave everything to me." Drugs lured us with a similar siren song. A favorite saying of an alcoholic friend of mine was, "Let's get drunk and be somebody."

It is especially dangerous when we start believing our own lies, as does Korach. Notice how he projects his own shortcomings onto Moses. He desperately desires to usurp Moses and Aaron's command, yet he alleges that it is *they* who "lift themselves up" over the people. He accuses Moses, the meekest man on the planet, of arrogance! He argues that they have taken on too much, but isn't it Korach himself who is blatantly overreaching?

Our own rebellions in life against God, responsibility, and others frequently arise because we are unwilling or unable to look at our own shortcomings. Whenever someone rubs us the wrong way, chances are that person shares a character defect with us that's a little too close for comfort. It is, of course, far easier to find fault with others than to fix ourselves. The problem is, finding fault with others doesn't do us any good. There are things in life worth struggling for. Today, we can pray for the wisdom to choose and the courage to win those battles that are for the sake of heaven.

Tuesday

**Korach guarded with peace. The one who guards with
peace guards with the Holy Name.**
Zohar V, 176a

Figure it out. Peace is the foundation of the world. And God
is the builder. When you threaten peace, you rise up against
God. And that's something you don't want to do. Stay cool.
Stay serene.

Wednesday

His very subtlety has led him into error.
Babylonian Talmud, Baba Metzia 96b

Don't be so clever and full of yourself. The only one you will
outsmart is yourself. Everyone else sees through it and you.
When you are that transparent, there's nothing left to see.

Thursday

And Korach . . . took . . .
Numbers 16:1

The Hebrew text does not indicate exactly what Korach *took*. Most translations assume it to be men, that is, his followers, but literally, the words can be understood as an open-ended, limitless taking. If some of us are givers, and others are takers, it is clear into which category Korach falls.

The Midrash tells us that Korach was one of the wealthiest men who ever lived, but that wasn't good enough. It ate him up inside that he was not as honored as Moses. It seems more than incidental that his punishment for rebelling against Moses and God was to be swallowed up by a hole in the ground.

Addiction can be like an insatiable black hole within us. Comparing ourselves to others is an almost surefire recipe for creating resentment, internal rebellion, and, ultimately, grief. It is but a short leap from feeling deprived to feeling entitled to right that perceived "wrong," no matter what—but that's just wounded pride gunning for revenge. Putting our wants ahead of the will of God is a form of rebellion, conscious or otherwise.

Anytime we feel a desperate longing for something that we don't have, it may be a good idea to ask ourselves why we want it so much. Serenity comes with the realization that what we have right now is enough.

Friday

O God, Source of the breath of all flesh! When one person sins, will You be wrathful with the whole community?
Numbers 16:22

Sometimes we think that others will lead us into sin. But they only lead us where we want to go. Keep yourself clean, and keep others clean by not leading them into sin.

Shabbat

**And the earth opened its mouth and swallowed
them up with their households.**

Numbers 16:22

There *is* reason to worry. The Bible states it rather clearly.
When you play with fire, you can get burned. Severely.
Korach threatened the authority of Moses, and the earth
swallowed him up. When you pop pills, you don't just swallow them, they swallow you. You become them. There's only
one way to prevent it. Stay away from pills—and anything
else that will lead you to wrongdoing. The Torah offers us
these metaphors to help us fashion our lives, and learn from
the foibles of those who have lived before us. Korach
becomes a symbol for rebellion. But there is more. Moses is
leading the Israelite people from slavery to freedom.
"Rebellion" thus means that Korach does not like the road
on which Moses is taking the people. It is too long, too
unwieldy. He wants shortcuts, to get there fast. Forty years
are necessary to transform the people. Similarly, for us, recovery takes time. We don't renew our lives overnight. *Teshuvah*
does not happen in an instant. Admitting that we are powerless over our addiction gets us on our way, but we still have a
long road to travel. The Torah understands the business of
recovery and renewal. It is not some wishy-washy book of
meaningless dribble. It teaches us the lessons of life, of sur-
vival. So learn from it. Don't get swallowed up like the
companions of Korach. Choose your protests carefully. Rebel
against the life you led. There, you can make changes that
make a difference. Korach was envious of Moses. Who
wouldn't be? But this jealousy literally consumed him. This
jealousy drove him to undermine what could have been
channeled into good works. That is what happens when our
drives and our calculations take control of our lives.

Questions for Self-Reflection

1. Do I continue to rebel against God?

2. How have I sought to protect my sanctuary?

Notes to Myself

Sacred Thoughts for Holy Living

If your impulse to evil begins to tempt and mock you, push it aside with words of Torah, and God will consider you as having created peace. Serenity will be your achievement.

Genesis Rabbah 22:6

For Renewal, A Psalm

But they went on sinning against You

Defying the Most High in the parched land.

To test God was in their mind

When they demanded food for themselves

They spoke against God.

God heard and raged . . .

Because they did not put their trust in God

Did not rely on Your deliverance.

Psalm 78:17-19, 21

A Prayer

O Adonai, as You turned the curse of Balaam into a blessing, so turn all our dreams into something good.

From the Siddur,
*recited between benedictions
in some congregations*

Personal Thoughts and Commitments
for
Self-Renewal This Week

Chukat: Mystery
Numbers 19:1-22:1

You are far, farther than the heaven of heavens and near, nearer than my body to me.

Bachya ben Asher, Kad Ha'kemach

- ✔ The ritual of the mysterious red heifer is described, as are the laws of purification that go with it.
- ✔ The forty years of wandering begin to wind down, as the deaths of Miriam and Aaron are recorded.
- ✔ It becomes clear that the generation who knew slavery in Egypt will not enter the Promised Land.
- ✔ The conquest of the land continues.

Sunday

If he fails to cleanse himself . . . he shall not be clean.
Numbers 19:12

Cleansing comes from the inside, not the outside. It's no real mystery. If you wait, it's just not going to happen. You have to do it yourself.

Monday

This is the statute of the law which Adonai has commanded, saying: Speak unto the children of Israel that they bring to you a red heifer . . .

Numbers 19:2

The red heifer statute is widely regarded as the most unfathomable of God's decrees. Its aim is to purify those defiled by contact with the dead, yet the red heifer paradoxically defiled all those connected in any way with its preparation.

According to the Rabbis, even the wise King Solomon was stumped by this law. He then said to himself, "If this is so, could it not be that the other commandments, whose reasons I thought I had discovered, may have other, more profound and mysterious purposes that have eluded my grasp?"

This gets to the heart of the matter. The statutes *(chukim)* are greater tests of our faith than the other commandments, simply because they don't always make sense. Thus, by observing them, we tacitly acknowledge our belief in a Higher Power's higher intelligence. As the Torah puts it, "Trust in God with your whole heart, and do not lean on your own understanding" (Proverbs 3:5).

Blind, unswerving obedience is not what recovery is about—but neither is rationalization. We cannot *think* ourselves clean (in fact, our "best thinking" is what got us here!) and, especially in early recovery, doing should preempt understanding. When you think about it, the very notion of recovery—addicts helping other addicts—seems preposterously illogical. We have learned that it is OK not to have all the answers. Today, let us humbly accept that there are limits to our understanding as well.

Tuesday

**The mixture of water and ashes reminds human beings of
what elements they are made. Knowledge of self is the
most wholesome form of purification.**

Philo of Alexandria

The mysterious mixture is just a symbol. On its own, it can't
do anything. With our mixing, it can do anything.

Wednesday

How God rules the universe . . . is a complete mystery.

Moses Maimonides,
Moreh Nevuchim, *I:72*

We don't have to know how it works. It is enough to know
that we can count on it to work. Once our faith in order has
been restored, we can go on with our recovery.

Thursday

**And God said " . . . speak to the rock before their eyes,
that it give forth water. . . ." And Moses lifted up his hand,
and smote the rock with his rod twice . . .**

Numbers 20:8, 11

This is Moses' sin, for which his punishment is that he will not enter the Promised Land. Exasperated at the continual complaining and relapses in the faith of his people, he angrily calls them "rebels" (Maimonides maintains that it is this harsh outburst that actually is Moses' sin) and then hits the rock, a striking example of displaced anger if there ever was one.

The good news is that God grades us on a curve. The bad news is that we don't know where we are on that curve—or maybe that's good news, too, because if we ever knew for sure that we were living up to God's expectations of us, we would probably stop right there, being the good addicts that we are. And, spiritually speaking, when we're coasting in neutral, we're probably going downhill.

According to Rabbi Samson Raphael Hirsch, "Judaism teaches that the greater the person, the stricter the standard by which that person is judged." And, since we are qualified to determine neither how "great" a person is nor by which standard he or she is to be judged, we would do well not to judge. Better to do our best to raise our own spiritual level, while keeping in mind that falling short is part of what it means to be human. Even Moses had a bad day or two.

Friday

Whatever the person touches is unclean.

Numbers 19:22

Sometimes it just seems that way. Whatever we do is wrong. Whatever we begin ends in failure. Even as we succeed, we seem to fail. Stay clean and change the pattern. Just believe in yourself, and you can do almost anything!

Shabbat

If anyone who is bitten looks at it, he shall recover.
Numbers 21:8

Like the mystery of the healing of those bitten by the fiery figures in the desert, such is the mystery of recovery. According to the Mishnah, it was not the fiery serpent that healed. Rather, as long as the Israelites looked upwards and subjected their hearts to God in heaven, they were healed. When they refused to do it, they were destroyed. We don't fully understand this, nor should we attempt to do so. Something happens, finally, and we awaken feeling reborn. Starting over is tough. It's like a baby learning to walk and talk for the first time. There's so much to learn. And, in the case of recovery, to *unlearn*. When we are hidden in the womblike comfort of an addiction, in the artificial world we create for ourselves, life seems simple. But real life is outside of the womb. And so is recovery. It is a wonderful mystery. Each breath we take is beyond our comprehension, even if we know how bodies work. That's where the real high is—in the air we breathe, the life we feel living inside of us. We are all finely tuned instruments, driven by a spark of the Divine. Even when we force that instrument to go out of whack by drink and drugs, God extends to us an open invitation to return. And, somehow, we are able to do so. We gather the strength and take the long walk home. We put our lives back in order. We stop using and abusing. That's the mystery—that we can do it.

Questions for Self-Reflection

1. How do I prepare for my years of wandering to come to an end?

2. What can I do to finally let go of the past and prepare for the future?

3. What is the source of my strength to continue my journey until I reach the Promised Land?

Notes to Myself

Sacred Thoughts for Holy Living

The secret things belong to God but the things revealed belong to us and to our children forever. The trouble is that even the revealed things are unseen by us.

Reuben Alkalai

For Renewal, A Hymn

How splendid is Your light which worlds do
  reflect.

My soul is worn for Your love's delight.

Please good God, do heal her, and show to her
  Your face.

So my soul can see You and bathe in Your grace.

There she will find strength and healing in this
  sight;

Her joy will be complete, then Eternal her delight.

From "Yedid Nefesh,"
generally chanted between Mincha and
Maariv on Friday evenings.
Translated by Zalman Schachter-Shalomi
in Hashir Ve'hashevach

A Prayer

Number me the days that are not yet come. Gather me the raindrops that are scattered. Make me the withered flower to bloom again.

From the Apocrypha, 2 Esdras 5:36

Personal Thoughts and Commitments
for
Self-Renewal This Week

Balak: Only Blessings
Numbers 22:2-25:9

There are two treasures of life:
Peace and blessing.
Babylonian Talmud, Hagigah 12b

✔ After accepting an invitation by King Balak of Moab to curse Israel, Balaam offers a blessing instead.

Sunday

Then Adonai uncovered Balaam's eyes.
Numbers 22:31

With our eyes closed to the world around us, we see nothing. It seems obvious. But, too often, we walk sightless, refusing to see our lives for what they have become. When God opens your eyes, you see the world for what it is—and what it can be.

Monday

**And Balak said to Balaam: What have you done
to me? I took thee to curse mine enemies and
behold, you have blessed them all.**
Numbers 23:10

Balaam sets out to destroy the people of Israel with words,
but then encounters the miracle of his talking ass, who
protests his repeated abuse, and the sword-bearing angel. He
decides, wisely, to change his curse to a blessing. One commentator says that it isn't so much this miracle that causes
Balaam's change of heart, as it is the numbers, power, and
unity of Israel that he subsequently witnesses.

Recovery is also a rather miraculous way of turning the curse
of addiction into a blessing and getting back into the main-
stream of life. We are fortunate to be in a place where such
spiritual 180-degree turnarounds happen every day. For
example, by sharing a story about the hopelessness and
degradation to which her drinking led her, a woman turns
her former pain into a group's gain; she affirms the message
that, no matter what other situations the group's members
are currently going through, at least they don't have to live
like that anymore.

Two recovery messages can be gained from Balaam's story:
One, when the angel of destruction is blocking our progress
through life, that's a strong signal that it's time to change our
direction. And, two, there is great, proactive spiritual power
in group unity for a good purpose. People may have some
difficulty believing in a talking ass—but, believe me, *I've* hal-
lucinated worse! What no one in recovery should have any
trouble believing in is the profound spiritual truth that curses
may be blessings in painfully good disguise.

Tuesday

The one who utters a blessing is blessed.
The one who utters a curse is cursed.
Ruth Rabbah 1:3

It's not automatic, something like you are what you say. Instead, it depends on whom we associate with. If we hang out with active alcoholics, our ability to enter recovery will be severely decreased. If we spend our time with those in recovery, we have a chance for our own recovery.

Wednesday

Hatred causes a person to forget his dignity.
Rashi (to Numbers 22:21)

Hatred is all-consuming. It is negative energy. It discolors our entire world. Like alcohol and chemicals, hatred literally eats away at our bodies and souls. If you can't yet love, start by not hating. That will be your blessing.

Thursday

How fair are your tents, O Jacob, Your dwellings, O Israel!
Numbers 24:5

This is the famous beginning of Balaam's third blessing. It has become the introductory morning prayer, said upon entering the synagogue. And although originally the comment was a spontaneous expression of admiration at the sight of the Israelite encampment—a holy people living in peace—it also provides us with a valuable insight into how serenity can be achieved in our own lives.

"Tents" easily can be seen as a symbol for one's interior space. How are things *within* us? How do we really feel? "Dwellings" similarly can be understood as our place in life. Are we satisfied with where we are? Are we free of resentment and envy of others? In short, are we living in peace with *ourselves?* If we are, then we already have one of the greatest blessings of all. And if we aren't—and are not willing to make our best effort to let go of our anger, hate, guilt, or other emotional or spiritual pain, then anyone's good wishes and blessings will just be so many hollow words. We will not be ready to receive them.

One of the greatest blessings of recovery is the discovery that what we focus on affects the way we feel. There is already an abundance of blessings in our life, if we are but ready to see them. Instead of feeling shortchanged because we don't get everything we want, why not appreciate all the things we don't get that we don't want?

Friday

Then Balaam set out on his journey back home.
Numbers 24:25

Only after he had uttered a blessing (three, in fact) could Balaam return home. Had he cursed the people of Israel, he probably would have remained in the wilderness. Blessings become the path of our journey home.

Shabbat

Don't curse them and don't bless them.
Numbers 23:25

Balak is furious. He asked Balaam to curse the Israelites and instead Balaam has blessed them. Balak tries once more to persuade Balaam to utter a curse. No way. That's the power of faith—when it courses through your blood, the words you utter, however intended, are transformed into blessing. Balaam is overcome by spiritual ecstasy. He is overpowered by the Divine spirit, with the kind of feeling that weakens the knees, robs the tongue of speech but emboldens the heart. The physical senses become numb. Only the eyes of the mind are fully open. If we experience the feeling once in our life-time, we may consider ourselves truly blessed. But seeing the Divine vision that one time is all it takes for our life to unfold in front of us, one day, every day, one day at a time. It's the same thing on Shabbat; when you believe, you rest, and that holy rest informs your entire week—and life. Shabbat is like a twenty-four-hour blessing. It bestows on us the rewards of holy rest. And you become the blessing in all that you do, in the life you lead.

Balak's plea to Balaam, neither to bless nor to curse, may be more applicable to us than to Balaam. In the context of spiri-tual renewal, do not judge yourself harshly. Neither overestimate nor underestimate who you are. We are neither *tzaddikim* nor sinners; we are human beings with problems, shortcomings, and strengths. When it comes to looking at our-selves, let's leave the blessing and the cursing to the One most qualified for the job. And accept yourself for who you are.

Questions for Self-Reflection

1. How can I turn those things in my life that I have cursed into blessings?

2. How shall I respond when I am asked to destroy my competition?

3. Shall I be silent while someone else curses, or will I gather the strength to speak out?

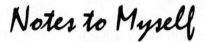

Notes to Myself

Sacred Thoughts for Holy Living

A traveler was passing through a desert and grew hungry, faint, and thirsty. He found a tree whose fruit was sweet, whose shade was pleasant, and at whose roots flowed a stream. After refreshing himself, he was about to take his leave when he said, "Tree, how shall I bless you? If I say to you, 'May your fruit be sweet,' it is already sweet. 'That your shade be pleasant,' it is pleasant now. 'That a stream should nourish you,' this is yours already. But I will say, 'May all the saplings planted from you be just like you.'"

Babylonian Talmud, Taanit 6a

For Renewal, A Psalm

He shall carry away a blessing from Adonai
Whatever is due to him, from his saving God.
Such are the type of people who have recourse to God,
The God of Jacob who seek Your favor.

Psalm 24:5-6

A Prayer

Help us, O God, to lie down in *shalom*
But teach us that *shalom* means more than quiet.
Remind us that if we are to have *shalom* at night
We must work our program during the day.
Grant us the *shalom* that comes from honesty so that no
 fear of discovery will haunt our sleep.
Rid us of hatred and resentments, which rob us of the
 shalom and serenity we seek.
Liberate us from our compulsive behavior, which disturbs
 us and gives us no rest.
May we inflict no pain, bring no shame, and seek no profit
 by another's loss.
May we so live, one day at a time, that we can face the
 whole world with serenity.
May we feel no remorse at night for our behavior during
 the day.

From "Hashkiveinu,"
JACS Friday evening service

Personal Thoughts and Commitments
for
Self-Renewal This Week

Pinchas: Zealotry

Numbers 25:10-30:1

Faith is not only in the heart. It also should be put into words.

Rabbi Nachman of Bratzlav

- ✔ As a result of the zealous "justice" meted out by Pinchas by punishing those who got involved with Moabite women and followed them to idolatry (at the end of the previous portion), Pinchas and his descendants are awarded a hereditary and permanent priesthood in Israel.
- ✔ The people are put on alert in the form of a second census.
- ✔ Moses prepares for his death; and Joshua prepares to succeed him.
- ✔ The sacrificial ritual for festivals is described.

Sunday

I grant him my covenant of peace.
Numbers 25:12

Unbridled zeal can lead you to do what Pinchas did. He was impatient and did what he thought Moses should have done. We are not comfortable with his action. Neither was God. That may be why God gave Pinchas a covenant of peace. He gave him serenity—so that he would not again be consumed by his zealotry.

Monday

**He was jealous for his God and made
atonement for the children of Israel.**

Numbers 25:13

Whatever the reader may think of Pinchas's bold and zealous act, the text makes clear that God finds it praiseworthy. The motives of Pinchas were absolutely pure and holy: The Midrash says that he was trying to avert a plague that ultimately killed 24,000 Israelites before his prayer stopped it; the Targum notes that Pinchas invoked Divine assistance through prayer even before performing his deed.

The Jewish view is that the individual not only has the right but also the obligation to speak up and act to uphold the will of God if it is being violated. In reality, of course, doing this usually is not easy or popular. People generally do not appreciate being told what to do—all the more so, if they are wrong. Especially in recovery meetings, where people of different backgrounds join together for a common good, we must avoid imposing our values on others. Managing someone else's recovery doesn't work. "Keep the focus on yourself" remains the best suggestion.

Nevertheless, even within the tolerant parameters of recovery, there are some behaviors that may threaten the group's welfare, for which swift and sure action is called. As in the Pinchas story, however, these are exceptional circumstances wherein the "fixer" is very clearly guided by a Higher Power. Most of the time, zeal and ego are a dangerous mix.

Tuesday

With faith, there are no questions. Without faith, there are no answers.

Chofetz Chaim

When zealotry becomes tempered by serene faith, religious passion is born, and the potential to do what Pinchas did is abated. And that's good. Questions are indispensable to faith. And answers, when articulated properly, resolve some doubt and bolster our faith. They also expand our religious knowledge so there are more things we want to know. Go out and seek truth. Maybe one day you'll find it.

Wednesday

The whole value of a benevolent deed lies in the love that inspired it.

Babylonian Talmud, Sukkah 49b

Deeds done for the wrong reason are not deeds at all. They are examples of stinking thinking, chess games with people as pawns. Do things out of a love for self, for others, and for God. That will sustain you and the deed you perform.

Thursday

**Pinchas . . . has turned my wrath away from
the children of Israel, in that he was very
jealous for My sake among them . . .**
Numbers 25:11

As a Jew, I am acutely aware of the countless horrors that
have been perpetrated against people in the name of God. It is
hard for me to respect Pinchas, much less to like him. I do not
doubt the sincerity of his intentions, just the consequences. It
seems to me that vigilantism, even Torah-condoned vigilantism, is not enough carrot and too much stick. Even the
Midrash doesn't say that Pinchas *had* to kill the illicit couple—just that it was permissible for him to do so. But
whatever happened to loving your neighbor as yourself?

Passages like these challenge my own understanding of what
Judaism and Torah principles are all about. What I would
like them to be more than occasionally conflicts with what
they are. That leave me confused, sometimes—but not at the
expense of my faith. My religious sensibility is flexible
enough so that a few loose twigs are not going to destroy the
tree. I can buy *most* of the package without feeling the need
to buy all of it. If that makes me a rebellious heretic, well . . .
the God of my understanding prefers honest disagreement to
blind obedience.

By a similar token, not everything you hear at meetings is
going to be worthwhile. Take what you need, leave the rest,
and pray for the wisdom to know the difference.

Friday

Take a census of the whole Israelite community.
Numbers 20:2

When Israel goes astray, God asks Moses to take a census. It
isn't a counting. Rather, it's a *recounting* of their life and
deeds. Take stock of yourself before you continue your journey, especially if you feel you have gone astray.

Shabbat

Ascend these heights of Abarim and view the Land that I have given the Israelite people.

Numbers 27:12

Moses finally knows for certain that he will never enter the Land that he has been journeying toward nearly his whole life. He could only go so far, and then he had to stop. Various teachers have speculated why. Was it really because he struck the rock twice, because he did not have faith in God's power? Was it because he remembered the slavery of his people and only those without that memory could be truly free? Disappointed, Moses ascends the mountain in order to see Canaan from afar and gain perspective on his entire life. In Joshua, Moses has raised up a leader who will take the people where he cannot go. But had Moses not led them to this point, Joshua could not take them further. They wouldn't be here.

It is often painful to let go of a sponsor or friend in recovery who means so much to us. Making spiritual renewal dependent on one person is not healthy. Recovery and renewal are our responsibility. In our spiritual lives, there will be many people who will lead us forward, but, at a certain point, they will stop, and we will have to go the rest of the way on our own. Keep walking.

Questions for Self-Reflection

1. How will I know when to act even when leaders do not?

2. How often shall I take an accounting of my life?

3. What have I done to prepare others to do what I now do when I must move on to other things?

Notes to Myself

Sacred Texts for Holy Living

In my youth, when I was fired with the love of God, I thought I would convert the whole world to God. But soon I discovered that it would be quite enough to convert the people who lived in my town, and I tried for a long time but did not succeed. Then I realized that my program was still too ambitious, and I concentrated on the people in my household. But I could not convert them either. Finally it dawned on me: I must work upon myself, so that I may give true service to God. But I did not accomplish even this.

Rabbi Chaim Halberstam

For Renewal, A Hymn

You guard the steps of Your faithful ones

But the wicked will be silenced in darkness,

For not by one's own strength shall an individual prevail.

They who fight with Adonai will be shattered,

Against their will You thunder from heaven.

Adonai brings judgment to the very ends of the earth.

Hannah's prayer, 1 Samuel 2:9-10

A Prayer

Rab declared, "We give thanks to You Adonai because we are able to give thanks."

Babylonian Talmud, Sota

Personal Thoughts and Commitments
for
Self-Renewal This Week

Mattot: Oaths
Numbers 30:2-32:42

"No" is an oath and "Yes" is an oath.
Babylonian Talmud, Shevuot 36a

- ✔ The power and the responsibility of taking oaths are discussed.
- ✔ Moses takes part in his last military enterprise.

Sunday

Do not move us across the Jordan.
Numbers 32:5

The land had been promised, and we journeyed toward it for what seemed an eternity. Yet, like so many other things in life, when we confront the reality of something that we have imagined for so long, we are scared. No blame. No shame. Just a human expression of fear. But God made a promise to them, an oath; that, you don't fool with.

Monday

When a person makes a vow to God . . . that person shall not break his word; he shall do according to all that he says.

Numbers 30:3

If we do not keep our promises, we are consorting with lies. We become less trustworthy to others—and to ourselves. The expression "break his word" in the Hebrew literally means "profane his word," suggesting that the violation of our words is a kind of spiritual defilement. Certainly, the disparity between vow and deed makes us feel more conflicted about who we *really* are: the "good-as-her-word" promise-maker or the "just-can't-help-it" promise-breaker?

As recovering people, we know painfully well how the wreckage of broken promises littered our lives with shame. So many vain oaths. So much vain living. If you can't keep your promises, more than your words are lost.

Rabbi Akiba said that vows are a fence to abstinence (Pirkei Avot 3:13). Indeed, our recovery from addiction is grounded in the very simple, very serious vow that, just for today, we will not use, no matter what. It is a vow that is worth reaffirming every day—and, unlike trivial vows (which the Midrash tells us are not only unnecessary, but also wrong), a matter of life and death. So long as we keep this particular vow, our recovery will keep us. Saying what we mean and meaning what we say is a more responsible, more honest, and more healthy way to live.

Tuesday

**The person who makes too many oaths will
be filled with iniquity.**

Ben Sira 23:11

In the ancient world, oaths were serious business. One's reputation, one's very life, was predicated on oaths taken. But when you take too many oaths, make too many promises, there's no way you can keep them all. Only do what you know you can do. Leave the next thing for next time.

Wednesday

Respect yourself in your purest emanation, your word.

Samson Raphael Hirsch, Nineteen Letters

We are what we do and what we say we'll do. And if we don't do what we say we'll do, we're less than we'd be had we not said we'd do it in the first place. Think about it. A person's name, reputation, is indeed more precious than fine oil. In this case, it's all in your hands.

Thursday

But if he shall make them [her vows] null and void after he has heard them, then he shall bear her iniquity.

Numbers 30:16

Only God always lives up to God's word, which may be the meaning of the Talmud's statement, "The seal of the Holy One is truth" (Shabbat 55a). Human beings, on the other hand, need an out—and the Torah does provide a procedure for having vows invalidated.

If someone takes an oath or a vow (in Jewish law, a vow involves an object, while an oath pertains to an activity) and then has second thoughts about it, he or she can go to a wise scholar or to three laypeople. They can absolve the person on the basis of a declaration that, at the time of making the vow, the person was not fully aware of all its implications.

If, by analogy, we can regard our commitment to recovery as a vow *(and* oath!), then it surely can be said that there will come times when our commitment will flag—when we will want out. The Torah teaches that we do not have the right to unilaterally violate our vows. We can choose to do so, of course, because we have free will, but it will be at our own spiritual expense.

Before violating our recovery, the program suggests that we call our sponsor or anyone in the program or go to a meeting and talk about it. "Thinking it through" is also a good way to prevent our recovery from becoming through. Being able to ask for help when you need it is not weakness—it is a sign of spiritual strength.

Friday

We will not return to our homes until every one of the Israelites is in possession of his portion.

Numbers 32:18

God made us a promise. None of us can go home until we are all home. Our recovery is our responsibility. But we thank God for our recovery by helping others find their way home. It's the Jewish way.

Shabbat

If a person makes a vow to Adonai or takes an oath imposing an obligation on himself, he shall not break his pledge. He shall carry out all that has crossed his lips.

Numbers 30:3

A vow is a promise to do. An obligation is a promise to abstain. When our lives are going well, we have a tendency to forget those promises we made to ourself, before God. It's human nature. But whatever we have promised to do—usually in times of sickness and adversity—we must especially remember to do. God's help is there whenever we need it. And we all need it. When you say you are going to do something, do it. When you say you are not going to do something, don't do it. It's that simple. How many times did you say you'd quit—just one more drink, one more sexual fling, one more spin at the roulette wheel? The Mishnah says, "One's word remains void until mouth and heart agree." When you've said it so many times, it no longer means anything. Let's rethink it this way: When you make a promise, remember that God is your witness and your strength. If you don't do what you say you were going to do, you fool yourself. Big deal! But you also face God. That *is* a big deal.

Break the pattern. Only make promises that you can keep. Intent is insufficient. Let the words cross your lips. And if you're not even ready for that, don't make any promises. Start easy. One commitment at a time. Work at it until you are sure you can fulfill it or are as close to completing it as possible. People depend on you. But more than that, you have to depend on yourself.

Questions for Self-Reflection

1. What can I do to make sure that I don't make promises I can't keep?

2. How can I face my own fears?

3. What commitments have I made that I want to call God to witness?

Notes to Myself

Sacred Thoughts for Holy Living

Before going to sleep each night, the Berdichever Rebbe would make a list of all the things he had intended to do that day but hadn't accomplished. He would then say, "Master of the Universe, I promise that tomorrow I will have the strength of will to carry out these tasks." The next night he would do the same thing, even though many of the items on his list repeatedly occurred, night after night. One evening, after returning home from Kol Nidre (Yom Kippur) services, he went through his nightly routine—but this time a heavenly voice admonished him: "You said the same thing yesterday." To which Rabbi Levi Yitzchak responded, "Yes, but tonight I *really* mean it."

For Renewal, A Psalm

You who have made me undergo many troubles and

Misfortunes will revive me again,

And raise me up from the depths of the earth.

You will grant me much greatness,

You will turn and comfort me.

Then I will acclaim You to the music of the lyre

For Your faithfulness, O my God;

I will sing a hymn to You with a harp,

O Holy One of Israel.

Psalm 71:20-22

A Prayer

Give Adonai each one his bread, each body what it needs.

Babylonian Talmud, Berachot 29b

Personal Thoughts and Commitments
for
Self-Renewal This Week

Masei: Boundaries

Numbers 33:1-36:13

The past lives in us, not we in the past.
David Ben-Gurion

✔ A review of the wanderings of the Israelites.
✔ Levitical cities of refuge.

Sunday

When you enter the land of Canaan, this is the land that shall fall to you as your portion, the land of Canaan with its various boundaries.
Numbers 34:1

Boundaries. My freedom ends where yours begins. Respect it, and remember it. Just don't try to cross it.

Monday

**. . . this shall be the land that shall become
yours for an inheritance, even the land of
Canaan, according to the borders thereof.**
Numbers 34:2

Just as the Torah sets forth explicit new rules circumscribing
virtually every aspect of human behavior to make the Jews a
holy people, so here are the borders of the Holy Land very
precisely established. From a Jewish perspective, this demar-
cation is quite significant, as there are certain commandments
that can only be fulfilled within Israel (the Sabbatical year, for
instance).

People in recovery also accept new boundaries: that any
drinking or drugging or certain foods or certain unhealthy
behavior patterns are no longer acceptable. That certain people and places are best avoided. That urges to use can stay
urges before becoming actions.

These new, self-imposed limitations at times may feel restric-
tive. We long for the cloudy days and blazing nights of our
days in the wilderness—but those rose-colored fantasies never
were quite real. Most likely, these longings are just our disease's seductive way of making us miss our misery. In fact, by
the time we made it into recovery, most of us were hurtling
headlong into the abyss.

A healthy awareness of our limitations actually frees us from
enslavement by our insatiable egos and the dangerously false
notion that we can do anything we want. We can, if we're
willing to work for it, have just about anything we want. We
just can't have *everything* we want. The key to living peace-
fully within the borders of our own inner space is to focus on
wanting what's right.

Tuesday

**Don't make a fence that is more important
than what a fence is.**

Genesis Rabbah 18:3

Recovery is not more important than recovery. Think about
it. The program helps us to place a fence around our addiction. Torah helps us to place a fence around our lives.

Wednesday

**If a person intends to perform a good deed
but is prevented from doing so, he is to be
treated as though he had done it.**

Babylonian Talmud, Kiddushin 40a

Motivation. Intent. Posture. It's all part of the journey, getting
us on the way to where we're going. The boundary between
intention and deed becomes blurred. They are the same.
Consider why before you do what needs to be done. Then
you go out and do it.

Thursday

For the children of Israel, and for the stranger and for the settler among them, shall these six cities be refuge.
Numbers 35:15

Six cities of refuge, where people who committed involuntary homicides can have automatic asylum, are ordained. What's unusual about these safety zones is that they are available to Jew and non-Jew alike. Without these cities, the lives of these accidental killers would have been in continual jeopardy, by any distraught relative of the deceased who wanted to seek revenge.

The cities of refuge are a way of halting the vicious cycle, of stopping the madness. The meeting rooms of recovery are safe places, too. They are temporary shelters from the storm—places where we can confide our joys and our pains to people who we know will understand.

In those rooms, it doesn't matter where we've been or who we are, only that we want to do something about our problem. What we learn inside these rooms gives us the experience, strength, and hope to carry our recovery forward into the "real" world, where there is more temptation, and less sensitivity. We can be thankful today for having these spiritual "safety zones" so readily available to us. They work wonders against the feelings of isolation and shame that kept us "out there" for so long.

Friday

This shall be your land as defined by its boundaries on all sides.
Numbers 34:12

It's good to know where you stand—from all sides. Boundaries provide us with perspective and help us to feel at home. So comfortable. So soothing.

Shabbat

**The towns that you assign the Levites shall
comprise the six cities of refuge which you
are to set aside for a manslayer to flee to.**

Numbers 35:6

Special boundaries are needed for special cases. Sometimes
we need protected space. Time to think, to put our lives back
together. Our need determines the nature of the environ-
ment—whether it be synagogue, Twelve Step program rooms,
in-patient care, or even the horned altar of the Levitical city
of refuge! It's no shame to be in need. That's why these
places were created—to help us return to who we are, to protect us from becoming someone we really don't want to be.

Find a place of refuge and call it your own. In Sifre, we find,
"It is a place which sanctifies the object." In a way. It is the
place which sanctifies us whether it be a Twelve Step meeting
room or the synagogue. Even better would be a Twelve Step
meeting in the synagogue. These are places of refuge—protected spaces which give us time so that we don't have to
watch our backs. Someone else is watching for us, at least for
a while. Shabbat works the same way. All we have to do is
not do. God will take care of the driving, at least for today.

149

Questions for Self-Reflection

1. How often shall I review my own journey in the wilderness?

2. Where shall I establish the boundaries of my life?

3. How can I make sure I don't tread on someone else's boundaries?

4. Where is my place of refuge?

Notes to Myself

Sacred Thoughts for Holy Living

If I am I because I am I and you are you because you are you, then I am I and you are you. But if I am I because you are you, and you are you because I am I, then I am not I and you are not you.

Menachem Mendl of Kotzk

For Renewal, A Psalm

Open the righteous gates to me

So that I may enter them and praise Adonai.

This is the gateway to Adonai,

The righteous shall enter through it.

I praise You. You have answered me.

You have become my deliverance.

Psalm 118:19-21

A Prayer

We have heard the song of God's praise

May we ever be in the blessed circle of God's faithful

Exalted is Adonai through all eternity.

You conferred Your love upon us

By entrusting us with Torah.

*Adapted from the "Akdamut," written by
Meir ben Yitzchak of Mayence and Worms,
originally used to introduce the public reading of the Targum*

Personal Thoughts and Commitments
for
Self-Renewal This Week

Devarim: People, Places, and Things

Deuteronomy 1:1-3:22

The Torah is the map of the world.
Tzadok Rabinowitz,
Tzidkat HaTzaddik

- ✔ This portion serves as a prologue for the entire book of Deuteronomy.
- ✔ As part of a life review, Moses reviews the history of Israel in the desert.

Sunday

**These are the words which Moses spoke to
all Israel beyond the Jordan . . .**
Deuteronomy 1:1

All the people, places, and things that made us into a people—all those ingredients made us into a person as well. A sum of experiences and genes, nurture and nature, to which we add our own unique contribution. Never before, never repeated. Us just the way we are.

Monday

And I instructed you at that time all the things which you should do.

Deuteronomy 1:18

"At that time"—and *for* all time. The Torah and the Twelve Steps both give us a program for healthier, more spiritual living. We may accept them, reject them, struggle with them, and grow with them, but there is a certain reassuring security in the knowledge that they are permanent and unchanging.

We live in a disposable age, full of convenience, plastic, and waste. Relationship not working? Toss it. Job too dull? Switch. Toys not titillating enough? Buy new ones. The problem is, no matter where you go or what you buy, you're still you.

People move in and out of our lives, places change, and things bring only temporary satisfaction that is more diversionary than deep. But spiritual principles are forever, and a more spiritually based lifestyle can keep us grounded and connected to something that transcends the ephemeral whirlwind of day-to-day affairs.

The words of the Torah are eternal. The principles of recovery are not some passing fad. Both can richly bless our lives with purpose, pattern, and peace.

Tuesday

**The summit is not to be found up there, but
here below—with us, inside us.**
Mordecai Joseph of Izbitz

Don't look for heroes, mountains, and great achievements.
They will elude you. Search out the simple treasures of life:
good, honest people, a place to call home, and a favorite
book. That's enough to reach the mountaintop.

Wednesday

**Nine *tzaddikim* do not make a minyan, but one
simple person joining them, completes the
minyan. "Truly in the multitude of the people is
the Sovereign's glory" (Proverbs 14:28).**
Rabbi Nachman of Bratzlav

Change your focus from greatness to simplicity. There, you
will find God and find yourself.

Thursday

Adonai our God spoke to us in Horeb, saying: "You have dwelled long enough at this mountain . . ."
Deuteronomy 1:6

Rabbi Kalman Halevi Epstein, an eighteenth-century Hasidic leader, offers this comment: When you were on the mountain, Adonai told you that you are not to look upon every obstacle and hindrance as an unconquerable mountain, but that you must surmount any obstacles that might stand in the way of your correct conduct.

The "real world" is not as friendly or forgiving a place as rehab or the Twelve Step meeting rooms, but it is where most of our life is going to be lived. Sooner or later, we must apply there what we learn about recovery. A good suggestion often made is to avoid the people, places, and things that we associated with during our active addiction. Unfortunately, they don't always avoid us! Just because we have committed to changing ourselves doesn't mean we can expect that the world, or others, will change for us.

But "easy does it" applies here, as well. Making mountains out of molehills makes them more difficult to climb.

Go outside for a breath of fresh air, call someone in the program, or pray for the serenity to make it through the situation. And remember: No person, place, or thing *makes* us do anything that we really don't want to do. As long as we have the Step Two in our lives, we are never alone.

Friday

God has watched over your wandering through this great wilderness. Adonai your God has been with you these past forty years. You have lacked nothing.
Deuteronomy 1:7

The one constant in our journey: the presence of God in our midst. We may not have always felt it or acknowledged it. Nonetheless, God was there—in the desert of Sinai and in the wilderness of today, as we continue our trek toward Canaan.

Shabbat

None other than Adonai your God who goes before you, will fight for you, just as God did for you in Egypt before your very eyes and in the wilderness where you saw how Adonai your God carried you, as a person carries a child, all the way that you traveled until you came to this place.

Deuteronomy 1:30-31

Every so often we step back from the tapestry of our life in order to gain perspective on it. Psychologists call it a "life review"—times when we take stock of what we are and where we've been, in order to know where we might want to go. Our tradition calls it *cheshbon hanefesh,* an accounting of the soul. We look at each aspect of our life, one by one. It's not an easy process. It's really hard work. But we're really the only ones who can do it. Once we see where we have gone wrong—and we all have gone wrong along our way—we try to realign our lives. Sometimes, it's a major event or an anticipation of an opportunity for advancement that moves us to want to initiate a life review. Sometimes, the motivation seems to come from nowhere. But first we have to identify everything. We wake up in the morning and say to ourselves: "It's time to reevaluate my priorities. It's time for change." But don't kid yourself. It's not coming from nowhere. It's coming from everywhere; you've simply been missing all the clues until finally God screams out at you, from inside your soul.

But don't wait so long. Make this *cheshbon hanefesh* part of your regular routine, like prayer. Take stock of your life journey and then get on with the business of walking its path. Take your cue from the desert journey of our ancestors. That's why it was written down, so that we would all learn from it. It is here where Jewish history—the joining of a spiritual and chronological history—becomes real for us and everyone around us. It is here where the journey—people, places, and things—of the ancient Israelites becomes our journey as well. We become them, because we are them.

Questions for Self-Reflection

1. Once I have reviewed my life's journey to this point, how do I make the necessary changes?

2. What can I do to make sure that I will stay on the right path in life now that I have found it?

3. How can I share my experience with others, so that they can learn from it?

Notes to Myself

Sacred Thoughts for Holy Living

And it is, yes, about the Jews who do not exist
in their stupors of alcohol and their fogs of uppers,
the wives with their eyes so black and blue
they come to the Seder in sunglasses,
the poor, yes, whose four cups are theirs,
have always been, shall always be,
because of the angels, the agents scattered
to the far stretches of Creation
who care.

From "Passover 1991," by
Danny Siegel

For Renewal, A Psalm

I turn my eyes to the mountains;
Where will my help come from?
My help comes from Adonai,
Maker of heaven and earth.
Adonai will guard you from all harm;
God will guard your life.
Adonai will watch over your comings and
goings now and always.

Psalm 121:1-2, 7-8

A Prayer

Praised are You, Ruler of the Universe, author of the work of creation.

Blessing said upon seeing a great mountain

Personal Thoughts and Commitments
for
Self-Renewal This Week

Va'etchanan: The Main Message

Deuteronomy 3:23–7:11

Every glory and wonder, every deep mystery and all beautiful wisdom are hidden in the Torah, sealed up in her treasures.

Nachmanides

✔ The basic requirement of the Israelite: Embody Torah in your daily life.

Sunday

But if you search there for Adonai your God, you will find God, if only you seek God with all your heart and soul—when you are in distress all these things have befallen you and, in the end, return to Adonai your God and obey God.

Deuteronomy 4:29-30

No matter how many ways we say it, the message comes out the same. The only road is the one that leads you out of your addictive behavior and toward God. As a result, you will regain your vision and your life and be renewed.

Monday

**And now, O Israel, hearken unto the statutes,
and unto the ordinances which I teach you, to do
them, that you may live . . .**
Deuteronomy 4:1

The main message of Torah *and* recovery: Ask not what your Higher Power can do for you, ask what you can do for your Higher Power. And not because God needs it, either (God was, is, and will be God with or without your help), but because *you do*, in order to live a healthy, fulfilling life.

The teaching of Torah is not for mere intellectual edification, but for the doing. Rabbi Chiya taught, "Someone who studies Torah but does not intend to perform *mitzvot*—it were better that he not even be created" (Leviticus Rabbah, Bechukotai 35:7).

The Torah teaches us how to live as Jews. Recovery teaches us how to live as addicts, alcoholics, codependents, and so on. The *mitzvot* and the steps can be seen as "lifelines" for the soul—deeds and principles to hold onto after we've let go of our arrogance and self-destructive patterns. We need only recall what a zombielike existence our unmanageable lives had become to appreciate the difference.

Like the children of Israel's double portion of manna on Fridays (so they wouldn't have to gather it on the Sabbath), we are twice blessed. Our Jewishness can enrich our recovery, and our recovery can strengthen our Jewishness.

Tuesday

If Torah is here, wisdom is here.
Mendele Mocher Seforim

You can't have one without the other. That's the Jewish way. Study Torah to become wise, or, if you're smart, do what the Torah requires of you.

Wednesday

The object of the whole Torah is that the individual should become a Torah himself.
Baal Shem Tov

Be Torah. That's the ultimate expression of a love for God. Let your life reflect its teachings, even while it illumines your life.

Thursday

Therefore take good heed to your souls . . .
Deuteronomy 4:15

Rabbi Joseph Karo, the great legal scholar and mystic, comments that the Hebrew for "take good heed" is in the passive conjugation and "your souls" is preceded, unusually, by a conjunction that literally means "for." Why is this? This verse is taken as the biblical basis for taking care of one's body and protecting one's health. It can more correctly be read as follows: "See that your body should be *protected* (a passive translation for "take good heed") *for* your souls"—that is, for the sake of your souls. Anything that hurts our bodies harms our souls.

Addictive behavior takes a physical toll as well as a spiritual one. It is one of the many ironies—or is it insanities?—of addiction that, despite our self-obsession, we stop caring for ourselves. One of the more visible signs of the enhanced self-esteem that recovery brings is when we start to care more about our appearance, our diet, and our physical fitness.

In the Jewish view, both our bodies and our souls are God's most precious gift to us and should be treated as such. In truth, who can really say where one ends and the other begins? But it is clear that doing whatever we feel like doing can be hazardous to both. Adopting healthy habits is very much in line with doing the right things. A walk in a park is good for your body—*and* your soul.

Friday

**Know therefore this day and keep in mind that
Adonai alone is God in heaven above and on earth
below. There is no other.**
Deuteronomy 4:39

In order to comprehend the message fully, one has to acknowledge the sender. Otherwise, the words are not fully clear. One God, one message.

Shabbat

Observe God's laws and instructions which I enjoin upon you this day, that it may go well with you and our children after you, and that you may long remain in the Land that Adonai your God is giving you for all time.

Deuteronomy 4:40

Here's where it really counts. Not only will the spiritual life be restored to you—once you return—but the disharmony that has eaten up your household will be transformed, as well. Finally, you will have something to give to those you love: *Shlemut* (wholeness), peace, tranquillity. You will have a home life that is not characterized by addiction and abuse but rather a home life that exemplifies the good life according to Jewish values. There are no guarantees in life, but this is about as close as you can get.

The ancient Israelites were reminded time and time again that, if they simply obeyed God's instructions, they would be led to a good life in a good land. Some interpret this equation as reward and punishment. But they miss the point. God's instructions are not just rules to live by. If you follow the *mitzvot,* you will live life to its fullest in a most profound way. Thus, they lead you to a good life. That's the reward. To always feel at home, comfortable, tranquil. I've been to Canaan, and I want to be home again, always.

Questions for Self-Reflection

1. What can I do to remind myself constantly of God's message to me?

2. How can I make sure that my daily routine is filled with Torah?

Notes to Myself

Sacred Thoughts for Holy Living

The first person did not know her completely nor will the last understand her fully, for her understanding is fuller than the sea and her counsel is greater than that of the deep.

Ben Sira 24:28

For Renewal, A Psalm

Your decrees are my delight, my intimate companions.

Make me understand the way of Your precepts, that I may study Your wondrous acts.

Your teaching is true.

Though anguish and distress come upon me, Your *mitzvot* are my delight.

Your righteous decrees are eternal, give me understanding that I might live.

Psalm 119:24, 27, 142-44

A Prayer

Open my heart to Your Torah, so that my soul may pursue Your precepts.

Babylonian Talmud, Berachot 17a

Personal Thoughts and Commitments
for
Self-Renewal This Week

Ekev: Life Review

Deuteronomy 7:12-11:25

The one who is truly wise lives out what he has learned.
Sifre to Deuteronomy

✔ The provisions for the conquest of Canaan are laid down.

✔ God advises Israel on its inner life for a more spiritual existence.

✔ Moses continues to remind the Israelites of their misdeeds in the hope that they will not repeat them.

✔ Israel will live a good life on a good level should it follow God's instructions for living.

Sunday

And if you obey these rules and faithfully observe them, Adonai your God will maintain for you the gracious covenant that God made as an oath with your ancestors.
Deuteronomy 7:12

The journey of the Israelites is nearing completion, or so it seems. They are merely leaving the wilderness. The journey is never really complete. So take a step back. Look where you've come from before you try to figure out where you are going.

Monday

... one does not live by bread only, but by everything that proceeds out of the mouth of God does one live.

Deuteronomy 8:3

Plain and simple: We are here because God wants us to be here. It is not only through food that our lives are sustained. As the blessing for going to the bathroom puts it, if but one of the many vessels in our bodies were clogged, we would perish. Life is indeed fragile.

Yet it also is remarkably resilient. Anyone who has ever done a fourth-step life review probably appreciates that truth better than most. If we're addicts or alcoholics, we've undoubtedly ingested enough poison to bring us to death's door more than once. If we're codependents or ACOAs (Adult Children of Alcoholics), we have endured shame and abuse of a different sort but are certainly no less miraculous for having survived.

Doing a fourth step does not lead to perfect self-understanding—our intelligence is not great enough for that—but it can give us a better sense of who we are and a deeper appreciation of the fact that we did not become that way overnight.

The children of Israel have to wander in the wilderness for forty years until they progress to the point where they can enter the Promised Land. It took a long time for us to deem ourselves worthy of recovery. Our fourth step can reveal that we simply chose the wrong direction in which to look for the right things. Today, we can be thankful that we know more about what we need to nourish ourselves—and where and how to get it.

Tuesday

**I know a person's way is not one's own. It is not in a
person to direct one's steps as one walks.**

Jeremiah 10:23

We are not in control. Lots of people and things have an
impact on our lives. But we are responsible nonetheless.

Wednesday

**If there is no judgment below, there can
be no judgment above.**

Deuteronomy Rabbah 5:5

Don't expect God to do the work for you. God helps—but
not until you are willing to help yourself. Probe deeply. Look
at yourself. God will hold the mirror.

Thursday

. . . from the day you went forth from the land of Egypt until coming to this place, you have been rebellious against God.

Deuteronomy 9:7

In this week's portion, Moses reviews the situations and events that have brought the Israelites to this point. It is the national equivalent of recovery's fourth step. Jewish tradition always has viewed a searching, honest self-scrutiny as an opportunity to draw closer to the Divine.

Honest self-examination is often a strange new experience for recovering people. Many of us have avoided "looking in the mirror" for years, clinging to the childish notion that if we couldn't see ourselves, no one else could, either. We may be fearful of all the pain and powerful feelings that rummaging through our past might kick up, but the fact is that not looking at it does more harm than good.

Facing who we are is the turning point of spiritual change and *teshuvah,* return. It reveals the good, the bad, and the ugly. It lets the shame out and the innocence back in. It lets us know in our heart of hearts that we are not depraved monsters in need of punishment, but flawed human beings in need of love. God already loves us. Now is the time to start loving ourselves . . . which begins with acceptance . . . which begins by seeing what is really there.

Friday

Remember the long way that Adonai your God has made you travel in the wilderness these past forty years, that God might test you by hardships to learn what was in your hearts, whether you would keep God's commandments or not.

Deuteronomy 8:2

Jews are a people of memory. We do what we do because it is right and because we remember the journey of our ancestors. They struggled so we wouldn't have to do so. But that's not always the way life works. We do have to struggle and then look at our struggle to see what we have gained.

Shabbat

And now, O Israel, what does Adonai your God demand of you? Only to revere Adonai your God, to walk only in Divine paths, to love God, and to serve Adonai, your God with all your heart and soul.

Deuteronomy 10:12

That's all there is to it. It's the whole purpose of the life review. Review your past. And figure out where you are going. The trick is how to realign your life. What do you have to do? After you have seen where you have been, you make changes. You really have no choice. Your past life got you nowhere. The insight of the text—different from what a secular society might tell you—is that you should reconnect through heart and soul with God. Twelve-steppers call it a Higher Power. That's the only way to really realign your life. The prescription for a good life is contained in only a few lines. It seems simple. But you have to choose to want to get there first. That's where heart and soul serve you. Even in the depths of your despair, the Divine spark embedded deep within you never goes out. It helps you return to the path of righteous living.

Use this text to remind you of what you have to do to stay clean—and what you have to keep doing to stay alive. Don't be embarrassed by the need of a constant reminder. That's why it's in the Torah. The ancient Israelites needed to be reminded and so do we, their descendants. Regardless of where you've been, try to walk on the path. Don't worry. We'll help you find your way.

Questions for Self-Reflection

1. What have I learned from my journey?

2. What can I share with others so that their journey is made easier?

3. How shall I steer the future direction of my journey?

Notes to Myself

Sacred Thoughts for Holy Living

Our passions are like travelers. At first they make a brief stay.
Then they are like guests who visit often. And then they turn
into tyrants who hold us in their power.

Babylonian Talmud, Sukkah 32b

For Recovery, A Psalm

What we have heard and known

And our ancestors have told us

We will not hide from their children

Telling to the generation to come the praises
of Adonai

And Your strength and the wondrous works
You have done.

Psalm 78:3-4

A Prayer

Do Your will, O God, in Heaven above and grant tranquillity
of spirit to those who revere You below.

Babylonian Talmud, Berachot 29b

Personal Thoughts and Commitments
for
Self-Renewal This Week

Re'eh: Vision

Deuteronomy 11:26-16:17

Vision looks inward and becomes duty.
Vision looks outward and becomes aspiration.
Vision looks upward and becomes faith.

Rabbi Stephen S. Wise

✔ The blessing and the curse are both set forth as conditions for living.

✔ Worship is centralized. All other altars and sanctuaries are to be destroyed.

✔ The nation is told: Obey the law as it is written. Don't add or subtract from it.

✔ A warning about false prophets.

✔ A reiteration about what it means to be a special people: tithes, social equality, dietary restrictions, and holy days.

Sunday

You shall not act at all as we now act here,
every individual as he pleases.

Deuteronomy 12:8

Even as you recognize the need for change and the progress in recovery you've made, know that there is always potential for further growth. Once you see where you are going, you will be able to get there.

Monday

Behold, I set before you this day a blessing and a curse.
Deuteronomy 11:26

In the Hebrew, the sentence begins in the second person singular—"Behold thou"—and then shifts to the plural "you." The Kotzker Rebbe explains it thus: What is set before "you," the many, is the same for all, that is, the blessing and the curse is equally applicable to everyone. However, when it comes to beholding them, each individual sees them in his or her own way. What she beholds depends on who she is.

To any situation, we bring our values, personality, and life experiences. As recovering people, the God of our understanding and our sense of spirituality is likely to be influenced by our Jewishness. Conversely, our Jewishness can be enriched and awakened by many of the new things we learn in recovery. This book is a testament to that.

As we grow spiritually, our views change. A common Twelve Step definition of insanity is repeating the same mistakes and expecting different results. The Sages in Pirkei Avot like to define wisdom as being able to learn something from everyone—I imagine that should especially include our own mistakes. Today, in recovery, the future looks better than it once did. Our spiritual vision has greatly improved.

Tuesday

**The traveler who keeps on is bound to
reach his destination.**

Mishlei Chachamim

Vision is motivation. Knowing where you are going helps to
get you there. Set your sights and then get on your way.

Wednesday

Where there is no vision, the people perish.

Proverbs 29:18

Without vision, you'll have no place to go and no way of getting there. Our people wanted to get to Canaan and struggled
to get there. Canaan is more than a plot of land; it is a state
of mind. And we're still trying to get there. Come join us on
our journey.

Thursday

After Adonai your God shall you walk, and God shall you fear, and God's commandments shall you keep, and to God's voice shall you hearken, and God shall you serve, and to God shall you cleave.

Deuteronomy 13:5

An almost identically worded line occurs in last week's portion (Deuteronomy 10:20). The main difference is that, here, it is repeated in the plural. Said the Gerer Rebbe: "Under normal circumstances, it is enough if a person fears and serves God individually. But in days when instigators and seducers are all over the place, a single soul may not be sufficient. He must join with other like-minded people to form a group to resist."

Sounds pretty much like the idea behind recovery groups to me. In all the dysfunctions dealt with in self-help groups, distorted thinking patterns led to self-destructive behavior patterns. Moreover, our thinking—our inner vision—can remain blurry long after we discontinue those unhealthy behaviors. It is wisely suggested that we deal with our occasional urges to use by "thinking it through"—that is, by envisioning the consequences. But, even there, our vision may be too focused on the short term, or we just may not be willing to look farther. It is at those times that we most need the group or the help of a fellow program member. Being able to listen to and benefit from the viewpoints of others helps us to avoid the risk of deluding ourselves.

Friday

Be careful to observe only that which I tell you: Do not add or subtract from it.

Deuteronomy 13:1

When life goes smoothly, and things begin to go our way, we relax our guard, take short cuts, or take on too much. And, crash! The Torah tells us clearly. There is one way to the good life, although the roads to get there are many. Stay on the road. And take it easy.

Shabbat

You shall have nothing but joy.
Deuteronomy 16:15

And that's all we have been looking for. But we have been looking in the wrong places for the wrong things. We thought life was empty and tried to fill it up . . . with sex, food, drugs. Somehow the hole got bigger, and then we fell into it. A black hole in space—beyond our comprehension, without an ending. And we kept falling. When you bottom out, as painful as it is, you have stopped falling and can begin to make the journey home. It's the full fall that's so frightening. But joy accompanies you on the road to recovery. Not just happiness, but genuine joy, a special feeling of being alive. You have survived, and now it's time to rediscover what it's like to be alive. Every time you take a breath, every time you get up in the morning, you know the feeling. And on Shabbat that joy is even more intense, because it is enhanced by a vision of messianic proportions. You don't see the future. Instead you experience boundless potential on Shabbat, the ultimate of what the world has to offer and beyond. When Shabbat really works, the experience of it transforms you, and you feel yourself closer to Heaven and even closer to yourself. And that's joy.

Is it possible to have nothing but joy in life? No, of course not. That's just what the lie of addiction wants us to believe. If we don't have joy in our life, it is as if we have nothing. And if we do have joy, then whatever else we have or do not have hardly matters.

Questions for Self-Reflection

1. What can I do to know which road leads me to the blessing in order to avoid the road that leads me to the curse?

2. How can I be a special person by being all that I can be?

3. How can I discern false prophecy?

Notes to Myself

Sacred Thoughts for Holy Living

God is not always silent and man is not always blind. In every man's life there are moments when there is a lifting of the veil at the horizon of the known, opening a sight of the eternal.

Abraham Joshua Heschel

For Renewal, A Psalm

The upright see it and are glad,

And all iniquity stops her mouth.

Whoever is wise, let him see these things

And let them consider the marvels of
    Adonai.

Psalm 107:42–43

A Prayer

Make us all one heart, God, so that together as one people we may move forward unafraid of the tests and challenges of the inscrutable years which lie ahead.

*From a prayer offered by
Rabbi Abba Hillel Silver*

Personal Thoughts and Commitments
for
Self-Renewal This Week

Shoftim:
Structure and Stability

Deuteronomy 16:18–21:9

Rabbi Elazar ben Azara taught: Without Torah, there can be no social order; without social order, there can be no Torah.

Pirkei Avot 3:21

✔ The Israelites are given instructions as to how to stabilize the community once they have entered the Promised Land.

✔ These laws are intended to raise Israel to a higher moral state.

Sunday

You must be wholehearted with Adonai your God.

Deuteronomy 18:13

The structure is simple. Be yourself before God. But be totally yourself. In return, God will give you the stability you need.

Monday

**Judges and officers shall you make for
yourself in all thy gates.**

Deuteronomy 16:18

The Torah commands that every town establish a court and
appoint officers. As a child, I never understood why in small
towns, some judges are "justices of the peace." Now I do.
Societies cannot exist too long or too well without some form
of law and order. One of the more serious indictments leveled
against our own society is that many people feel that our
legal system is out of control. Civilization and civil law seem
to go hand-in-hand.

Some of us whose drug experiences began in the cultural context of the sixties didn't always think so. We thought that
rules were inherently oppressive, that any inhibition at all was
unhealthy, and that love, not law, was the kinder, gentler path-
way to peace. But if addiction taught us nothing else, it's that
some rules *are* for our own good. On both a social and personal level, healthy laws can preserve and promote the peace.

Meetings are a major way that recovering people can preserve and protect their inner peace, and they should be widely
available for all who want them. But sometimes they're not.
If you're in that situation, maybe you can be half of the solution. According to recovery tradition, it only takes two
people to start a meeting. Greater things have begun from
less. According to Jewish tradition, Judaism needed only one
person to start. His name was Abraham.

Tuesday

The impulses of a person are stronger within him in proportion to his greatness among his fellows.

Sukkah 52

After a person realizes the weaknesses that make that individual whole, he or she can confront them head on. No one is exempt, regardless of where he or she is in relationship to his or her neighbor. You may have achieved more, but remember that the *yetzer hara,* the evil inclination, that drove you this far has a dark side which is also large.

Wednesday

Rabbi Yochanan said, "If the teacher resembles an angel of God, seek Torah from him."

Babylonian Talmud, Moed Katan 17a

Everyone has something to teach you, and you can learn from all. But there is a difference between learning real Torah and simply learning from the experiences of life. Seek out a teacher, a sponsor. Don't wait for one to come running to you.

Thursday

Justice, justice shall you follow, so you may live . . .
Deuteronomy 16:20

The Hebrew root for the word "justice"—*tzedek*—also means "right." A variant of the word, *tzeedek*, means "justify," or "make right." That is the Jewish sense of justice: If something is wrong, make it right; if something is right, keep it right. Judgment is not so much to punish as to preserve the peace and integrity of society. Perhaps that is the ultimate purpose of our creation—to make the world a more righteous place.

We who find it so easy to judge others usually dislike being judged ourselves. And we who are in recovery are more apt than most to chafe under the yoke of someone else's rules. Nevertheless, and as much as we might wish otherwise, we have a conscience. In our hearts, if we are willing to listen, we usually know the difference between right and wrong.

The Torah and the principles of recovery speak in one voice on this: To fully *live* (that is, to avoid a psychologically, emotionally, and spiritually constricted existence), we need to shift our emphasis from doing what we want to doing what is *right*. Our evil inclination may whisper otherwise, but we must insistently reply, "Justice, *justice*. . . ."

Friday

It is Adonai your God who leads you in battle for you against your enemy, to bring you victory.
Deuteronomy 20:4

The enemy is addiction. The battlefield is inside yourself. Defeat it. That will bring stability back into your life.

Shabbat

You must not destroy . . .
Deuteronomy 20:19

Baal tashchit, not to destroy—this is not just a moral instruction for the ancient Israelites as they went to war. It is a basic Jewish moral imperative that provides a foundation for all that we do. It is what separates us as individuals and as a people. Like God who is Creator of all that we see and do not see, we seek to build, not to destroy. We already have seen too much destruction in our life—and we caused too much of it. We recognize that reality and are trying to live with that recognition. Thus this can be read as a directive to you as you fight your addiction. The *yetzer hara,* what the rabbis call your inclination to do evil, is one of the natural urges that is part of you. It's the dark, destructive side, so be careful of it—but don't destroy it. With it goes a large part of you.

If you regain structure and stability in your life—what a return to Judaism and a Twelve Step program offer you—you will remove the *yetzer hara*'s destructive power over it. You will regain control over your life. You will be renewed.

Shabbat is an important part of such a program. It is a part of Jewish life. As we struggle all week long through the seeming chaos of our workaday world, Shabbat comes each week to remind us that there is purpose and direction in our lives and in the world. With that reminder, we are able to see this direction and purpose more clearly throughout the days that follow. That's the special power of Shabbat. It provides us with a strength with which to manage the world around us, no matter how chaotic it may seem.

Questions for Self-Reflection

1. What do I need to do to reestablish order in my life?

2. How can I be sure that all I do has a moral standard?

3. What should I do to keep the message of *"baal tash-chit"* active in even the simple things that I do?

Notes to Myself

Sacred Thoughts for Holy Living

Turn, turn away, do not touch anything that
    is unclean
As you depart from there
Keep clean, as you depart from there
You who are vessels of Adonai.

For you will not depart quickly
Nor will you leave in flight,
For Adonai is marching before you;
The God of Israel is your rear guard.

Isaiah 52:11-12
Shoftim Haftarah

For Recovery, A Psalm

Surely God is good to Israel
Even to such as are pure in heart.
But as for me, my feet were almost gone
My steps had nearly slipped.
For I was envious of the arrogant
When I saw the prosperity of the wicked.
[But] pride is as a chain about their neck.
Violence covers them like a garment.

Psalm 73:1-3, 6

A Prayer

Blessed is my Higher Power whose love and compassion has
    led me to fellowship.
Blessed is the Compassionate One who has given me a pro-
    gram that has changed my life.
Blessed is the Master of the Universe who gave me Twelve
    Steps to live by.
Blessed is the Sovereign One to whom our praise is due.
Blessed is the Holy One who inspired those who gave us a
    program of recovery.
Blessed are those who came before us and showed us the way.

Adapted from the morning blessings,
JACS Foundation Shabbat morning worship service

Personal Thoughts and Commitments
for
Self-Renewal This Week

Ki Tetze: Entering Society

Deuteronomy 21:10-25:19

All Israelites are mutually accountable to each other.

Babylonian Talmud, Shevuot 39a

✔ Included in this portion is a diverse series of laws, all designed to imprint the social structure, described in the previous portion, with moral stature.

✔ Especially in the administration of civil and criminal law, Israel is instructed to be unlike the other nations.

Sunday

Thus you will sweep evil away from your midst.
Deuteronomy 22:21

Once into recovery—no matter how long you have been clean—you have to stay away from whatever can bring you down, in order to maintain a normal life, whatever that means. Don't be a hero. Just stay away from temptation. That's where evil lurks.

Monday

. . . you shall restore it [a lost farm animal] to him. And so shall you do with his ass; and so shall you do with his garment; and so shall you do with every last thing of your brother's . . .

Deuteronomy 22:2-3

Jewish law obliges us to return lost items—all the more so if they were stolen. An important part of our recovery involves acknowledging that we have harmed others, becoming willing to make amends to them all, and making those amends. This restitution helps reconcile our past with our present, not just in word and thought, but in deed. It is a powerful form of atonement. And it works.

The traditional argument for the legalization of certain "vice activities" such as drugs, gambling, or prostitution is that they are "victimless crimes"—but any addict knows better. We may have been the major victims of our self-destructive activities, but we certainly weren't the only ones. Lies and stealing, in one form or another, seem to be common twin indicators that our lives had become unmanageable. There is no guarantee that we can retrieve and restore all the relationships that our untrustworthiness damaged. All we can do is try.

It is sometimes said that recovery is a selfish program, but I do not agree. It is impossible to start respecting ourselves without having equal respect for the property, rights, and feelings of others. Part of recovery, an important part, is constructively coming to terms with the damage we have done to others and to society. Today, we can better appreciate that we hurt ourselves when we hurt others and hurt others when we hurt ourselves. In Judaism, there is no such thing as a victimless crime.

Tuesday

This world is an inn. The world-to-come is your home.
Babylonian Talmud, Moed Katan 9b

Just as we awaken each day with a renewed soul, according to Jewish tradition, we also reenter society with each morning sunrise. Each day we are given a chance to start over, to begin again. But we have to act on the opportunity given us. This world is real. Live it the best you can. In doing so, you can work toward a time of ultimate redemption.

Wednesday

The Torah is like a goad, because it serves to guide its students on their way.
Babylonian Talmud, Hagigah 3b

No matter where we turn or what we do, Torah serves us as the most perfect guide for living our lives in accord with the way God wants us to live. But Torah is more than a guide. It actually motivates us to do what is right because it holds the ultimate promise of redemption, of reaching closer to God.

Thursday

**When you gather the grapes of your vineyard, you shall
not glean it after you; it shall be for the stranger, for the
fatherless, and for the widow. And you shall remember
that you were a slave in Egypt; therefore I command
you to do this thing.**

Deuteronomy 24:21-22

Those who owned fields or vineyards in Israel were required
to set aside the produce at the corners of the field. If some
stalks of grain or a few grapes were dropped during harvest,
they had to be left on the ground for the poor to collect. And,
if a farmer forgot sheaves in the field, or if undeveloped grape
clusters were left unpicked, they too belonged to the poor.

Unlike the Torah's many statutes whose reasons are not
given, the purpose behind these laws is explicit: "You were
slaves, so have a little *rachmonis* (mercy)," God seems to be
saying. "Anyway, your crops are not all yours. I helped you
grow them, didn't I? The poor need to eat too!"

The relevant recovery slogan: You can't keep what you have
unless you give it away. Or at least some of it. We learn at
every meeting how helping someone else in recovery helps
our own recovery. Recovery cannot be stashed away nor
savored in isolation. It is meant to be shared. As we grow
spiritually, we are more able and more willing to reach out to
the newcomer. In general, we become more helpful, responsible, healthy people.

From the corners of our "recovery field," all the people in
our lives can reap some benefit. We learn that we have something of value to offer others—ourselves. Imagine that!

Friday

Let your camp be holy . . .
Deuteronomy 23:15

Society is not always as great as we would like it to be. That's
all the more reason why our homes need to be "small sanctuaries." From there we can build holy communities. But until
then . . . just make sure that you make your home a place for
God to dwell.

Shabbat

Always remember that you were a slave in Egypt; therefore do I require you to observe this instruction.
Deuteronomy 24:22

For the Jewish people nearly everything comes down to memory. Not only do we do things because God has instructed us to do them—and we know them to be right—but also because we know what it feels like to be at the short end of the rope. It's not a fun place to be. You can drown. We've been there, as a people in Egypt, as slaves to our addictions. And when we forget, we are reminded about what it was like.

That memory of "Egypt" shapes our personal memory as well. Maybe that's why, once we are in recovery, we stay close to those who feel the same pain, who know what it really feels like. But, remember, we were all slaves in Egypt. In a mystical, metaphysical sort of way, we were *all* there. And so we *all* share the same pain. I guess in a way, we are all in recovery together, former slaves and addicts alike.

While we may be creatures of habit, we are also creatures of choice, of free will. Slavery and addiction rob us of that. We are free today to remember what it was like in slavery. Real slaves can't—they are stuck in the mire. When life seems overwhelming, we've learned what to do: We pray, we let go.

Questions for Self-Reflection

1. What obligations do I have to myself as a former slave in Egypt?

2. What makes me different from others in the way I live my life?

3. How have I in some small way truly made this world a better place to live?

Notes to Myself

Sacred Thoughts for Holy Living

These are the things, the fruit of which a person enjoys in this world, while the principal is held for that person in the Olam Haba [the world to come]: Honoring one's parents, loving deeds of kindness, making peace between an individual and his neighbor, and the study of Torah, which is equal to them all.

Mishnah Pe'ah 1:1

For Recovery, A Psalm

Do not trust in oppression.

And do not put vain hope in robbery.

If riches increase, do not set your heart on it.

God has spoken once,

Twice I have heard it.

Strength belongs to God,

Also to You, God, belongs mercy

For You render to each person according to his deeds.

Psalm 62: 11-13

A Prayer

Rab Judah, after recovering from illness, was visited by Rab Hanan of Bagdad and other rabbis.

They said, "Blessed be the Compassionate One, who returned you to us and not to the earth."

He said, "Amen." Then he said to them, "My response is sufficient to fulfill the duty of giving thanks."

Babylonian Talmud, Berachot 54b

Personal Thoughts and Commitments
for
Self-Renewal This Week

Ki Tavo: Transformation

Deuteronomy 26:1–29:8

Today you have become the people of Adonai, your God.

Deuteronomy 27:9

✔ Continuing from the last portion, this parasha completes the numerous religious concerns of building a community.

✔ Another promise: Follow the instructions of Adonai, and you will be transformed into a holy person.

✔ You are in control of your destiny, as a partner with God. There are blessings and curses: You make the choice.

✔ As he prepares to turn over the reigns of leadership, Moses begins his final address to the people.

Sunday

And Adonai has affirmed this day that you are . . . a holy people.

Deuteronomy 26:18-19

Both recovery and spiritual renewal, together or separately, are transformative experiences. Neither turns us into different people. They simply return us back to our Source, so that we can once again become the individuals we always had the potential to be. Thus we become holy—"wholly separate" from previous lives and the lies we lived.

Monday

And you shall rejoice in all the good which Adonai your God has given to you, and to your house, and the Levite, and the stranger in your midst.

Deuteronomy 26:11

The main characteristics of addictive behavior are short-term pleasure at the expense of long-term misery, and a pervasive feeling of emptiness or deprivation. We mistake pleasure for satisfaction, and it doesn't work. That is why "one is too many, and a thousand never enough." Once the "thousand" is used up, as it inevitably will be, we are more miserable than ever. And doing "just one" sets off the whole awful cycle all over again.

The transformation that recovery brings is mainly one of attitude. Instead of wanting what we can't or don't have, we start appreciating all that we can and do have. We start taking less for granted. As our sense of self-worth grows, we even become less covetous and begrudging of the achievements and possessions of our fellow human beings.

With our faith in a Higher Power restored, we become aware that our true needs are being met, or, with the help of our Higher Power, will be met, and so we start to become less needy and more grateful. The less needy we are, the more giving we can be. Thus does recovery transform deprivation into delight. For, if we have God in our lives, what is it we truly lack? And, if we don't, what is it we really have?

Tuesday

Repentance makes a person a new creature; previously dead through sin, he is fashioned afresh.

Babylonian Talmud, Avodah Zarah 9a

Repentance is an amazing process. It allows us to become truly human, sparked by the Divine in us all. But we don't get there by saying we want to be there. We have to change our lives before our lives can change us. Move away from the alcohol, drugs, sex, food, and gambling—they are all dead ends. Fashion a new life out of the old. Giving birth to a new self is an awesome experience.

Wednesday

A twinge of conscience in a person's heart is better than all the floggings he may receive.

Babylonian Talmud, Berachot 7a

Sometimes we think we have to beat ourselves in order to make us change our lifestyles and lives. After all, it does say, "Spare the rod and spoil the child." Forget it. Hugs don't hurt.

Thursday

**These shall stand upon Mount Gerizim to bless the people . . .
and these shall stand upon Mount Ebal for the curse. . . .**
Deuteronomy 27:12-13

A life-or-death choice is set before the children of Israel. Half
the tribes stand on one mountain, half the tribes on the other.
The priests stand around the Ark at a midway point in the
valley. They first turn towards Gerizim and pronounce a
blessing, to which the entire multitude answers a resounding
Amen. Turning then to Ebal, they pronounce the correspond-
ing curse, which is followed by the same group response.

And what is the first blessing and curse uttered? "Blessed be
the person who does not make idols. Cursed be the person
who does." It is just as at Sinai: "You shall have no other
gods before Me." Except that we are further from Sinai now.
We no longer hear God's voice quite so clearly. Our own
thoughts and desires get in the way. We have choices to
make, choices that are neither clear nor easy.

The most important choice we make in recovery every day is
whether or not to accept God as our Higher Power or to give
ourselves over, again, to that substance or unhealthy behavior
that already has made us slaves. Everything else flows from
it—all the milk and all the honey. If we keep that choice
clearly before us, it is clear what to choose. Each day in
recovery is another blessing.

Friday

And all the people shall respond, *Amen*.
Deuteronomy 27:15

Change is dialogue. Moving from who we were to who we
want to be is a process of change with us in the middle. Each
step along the process demands our assent: *Amen,* so be it.
And then we move to the next step along our journey,
already different from who we used to be. Such power in
such a simple word. Thank God, I want to be here. *Amen!*

Shabbat

And all the blessings shall come upon you and take effect. . . . Blessed shall you be in your comings and blessed shall you be in your goings.

Deuteronomy 28:2, 6

You don't have to worry if you can't tell whether you are coming or going—because you will be blessed regardless. Just keep looking forward and walking that way. Don't long for the fleshpots of Egypt. You left them far behind. We recognize that spiritual advance is not a one-directional experience. And neither is recovery. Each step forward does not become easier. You are simply more surefooted, because you are farther away from the addiction you left behind. But each clean step you take means that you have much more to risk.

We don't want to deceive you. The process is transformational. But it is not easy. If it were easy, perhaps it would not be so worthwhile. You will have lapses; we all do. Remember what happened to the Israelites in the desert. Each time something went wrong or perhaps wasn't perfectly right, they were ready to call it quits, to go all the way back to Egypt— even after they had gotten more than halfway to the Promised Land. It is not coincidental that God took them the long way around. Forty years is a long time to get from Egypt to Israel—even on foot. It's all part of becoming better people. But these setbacks, too, are transformational. They continue to reveal our weaknesses to us so that when we realign our lives, we do so each time with more surety.

Go ahead. Get out of your addiction. Don't be afraid to leave. You will be blessed in your goings. And come back home. You're welcome here. You will be blessed in your comings. Back and forth, like a Jew at prayer, is the special movement of recovery and renewal.

Questions for Self-Reflection

1. What can I do to raise my life to a level of holiness?

2. What contribution to the building of community have I made?

3. Have I kept up my partnership with God?

Notes to Myself

Sacred Thoughts for Holy Living

Rabbi Eliezer ben Hyrcanus said, "Repent one day before your death." His disciples asked him, "How is it possible for a person to repent one day before his death, since he does not know on what day he will die?" He replied: "So much the more reason is there that he should repent every day, lest he die the next day. Thus will all his days be penitential ones."

Avot de Rabbi Natan 15

For Recovery, A Hymn

Glory in God's holy name

Let the heart of them rejoice who seek Adonai

Seek Adonai and Divine strength

Seek God's face continually.

1 Chronicles 16:10-11

A Prayer

Look down from your abode, from heaven, and bless me, one of your holy people Israel and the dirt that you have given me so that I might transform my life into one flowing with milk and honey—as you swore to my ancestors.

Adapted from Deuteronomy 26:15

Personal Thoughts and Commitments
for
Self-Renewal This Week

Nitzavim: Standing Firm, Standing Together

Deuteronomy 29:9-30:20

Among the great sages of Israel were wood-cutters, water-drawers and blind people.

Maimonides, Hilchot Talmud Torah 1:2

✔ In his final address, Moses recounts the wonderment of God's deeds.

✔ Moses instructs the Israelites to be loyal to God.

✔ Finally, Moses says, the Israelites understand the full extent of God's works and the special requirements of the covenantal relationship.

Sunday

Concealed acts concern Adonai your God; but with overt acts, it is for us and our children ever to apply all the provisions of this teaching.

Deuteronomy 29:28

The Torah deals with the overt, not the hidden. It is within the grasp of all of us to understand it. Reach out, and it's yours—but you have to reach out.

Monday

**You are standing this day, all of you,
before Adonai your God.**

Deuteronomy 29:9

Rashi comments that, when Israel heard the ninety-eight curses proclaimed in last week's Torah portion, their faces turned pale, and they despaired: "Who could possibly stand up against these?" For this reason, Moses began to calm them, saying: "Behold, you are standing, this day, all of you."

Sometimes it feels as if we can't stand it any more—we just have to use. Sometimes we may even say, "I can't stand it." Yet the fact is, as long as we're not using, we *are* withstanding it. Maybe we *wish* we weren't, maybe it *feels* as if we are about to cave in—but feelings aren't facts. When we feel at the end of our rope, it is especially tempting to crave instant relief, but we need to remember: Giving in to that feeling will topple us. Opening up the Pandora's box of active addiction is what we truly can't stand.

And that's when it is more important than ever to stay connected to your friends in the fellowship. One of the reasons recovery works is because it is impossible for everybody to have a bad day at once. We can help pick each other up and make it through the hard days. Bad days, hurt feelings, pain, and grief eventually fade. Getting through them, together, without using, strengthens our recovery—and ourselves. Hanging out together is a healthy alternative to "hanging ourselves" alone.

Tuesday

**As I live, declares Adonai, God—I *will* reign over you . . .
and I *will* bring you into the bond of covenant.**

Ezekiel 20:33, 37

It's a promise. If you can stand firm—and God will help you
to do so—then you will be able to stand together as part of a
fellowship with family and friends. That special sense of God
above you and beside you is part of the unique relationship
you share with the Almighty as part of the ancient covenant,
which you renew with your life and how you live it.

Wednesday

**When you walk, it will lead you. When you
lie down, it will watch over you. And when
you awake, it will talk to you.**

Proverbs 6:22

Now that's stability. It is also very comforting. But that is
what Torah is all about. Torah is like nothing else in your life.
"It is a tree of life for those who cling to it." It is a lifetime
companion. Seek out its message.

Thursday

See, I have set before you this day life and good, and death and evil . . . therefore, choose life . . .
Deuteronomy 30:15, 19

For those of us in recovery, this line rings especially true. We know where *not* being in recovery put us. We know that we are capable of returning to that sorry state. We know that we have a choice.

Of course on some days that choice is more clear than on others. This verse, for example, echoes Deuteronomy 11:26, which speaks of "a blessing and a curse" set before the children of Israel "this day" but does not go so far as to mention "life and good" or "death and evil." According to Rabbi Simcha Meir Hakohen, the reason for this section's more dramatic phrasing is that it deals with repentance. Failing to repent is a much more serious transgression than the sin that was committed originally. It is worse than a curse; it is evil, it is death. As Rabbi Simcha Bunam put it, "Failure to repent is much worse than sin. A man may have sinned for but a moment, but he may fail to repent of it moments without number."

Recovery is a form of repentance, and it, too, is for the highest of stakes. It must, therefore, remain our Number One priority, because to lose it is to risk losing everything. When life gets too complicated, when our commitment starts to wane, we need to talk about it, we need a meeting, and we need to remember: We do not go to meetings as a hobby or social outlet; we are in recovery for life.

Friday

I shall have peace though I walk in the stubbornness of my heart.
Deuteronomy 3:18

No way! If we fight it, we can't have peace. This text expresses a commitment. Even though we may fight it, Torah still holds the promise to provide us with the serenity of spirit that we all desperately seek. Don't fight it. Get back on the road to recovery. And return to God.

Shabbat

I make this covenant, with all its sanctions, not with you alone, but both with those who are standing here with us this day before Adonai your God and with those who are not with us this day.

Deuteronomy 29:13-14

Rosh Hashanah reminds us of our limitations. We like to imagine that "where there's a will, there's a way," but we know better. All too often, it is mere self-delusion to suppose that our destiny is completely under our own control, if only we make a sound decision, expend some extra effort, and do the right thing. Jews may be especially susceptible to the seductive illusion that we are masters of our own fate. Our culture has valued such things as hard work, getting ahead, and sacrificing for tomorrow—and, by and large, at least here in America, the strategy has paid off. No wonder we think we can do anything we want.

This Shabbat reminds us that we cannot hope to go through life bestowing unlimited blessings on those we love. We have the right to get tired, we will sometimes fail, we need help. Shabbat underscores that message. Sometimes we are dependent on God to do what we cannot. Millions of Americans are in Twelve Step recovery programs, admitting that they have "let go and let God." Millions more would do anything to cure a child of leukemia, to bring back a teenage runaway, to save a marriage. And there may be nothing they can do.

The real heroes of this world are not the people who claw their way to the top as if they were immune to the rule that says there are limits to human energy, human competence, and success. Forget the media's adulation of the brave and the beautiful, the rich and the powerful. The men and women who would make the front cover of any magazine I published would be the ordinary souls who muster the courage to go on, day after day, week after week, knowing they cannot solve life's worst problems but committed nonetheless to solving what they can. This Rosh Hashanah, they may be at services recalling that only God can bless the month (and the year) that is just beginning; and as they pause to think through the year just passed, they may find welling up inside them newfound fortitude and confidence that at least they will be able to bless the rest of the months, one by one. They will know the truth of the prayer that we say as Yom Kippur draws to an end: "God reaches out a hand" to us on these High Holy Days. We are not alone.

Rabbi Lawrence Hoffman

Questions for Self-Reflection

1. What can I do to keep God's works constantly in mind?

2. How shall I continue to be loyal to the covenant and live my life in its shelter?

3. How can I try to understand God's actions in my life?

Notes to Myself

Sacred Thoughts for Holy Living

Nature Pursues its Own Course

I do not believe that sickness is a Divine punishment
a malediction thrust down upon me from above
a chastisement meant to correct some transgression.
I do not believe that sickness is some mysterious test
a strange compensation designed to build character.

Rabbi Harold M. Schulweis

For Recovery, A Hymn

I will make mention of the mercies of Adonai

And the praises of Adonai

According to all that Adonai has bestowed on us.

And the great goodness to the house of Israel.

Which God bestowed on them according to Divine
compassion

And according to the multitude of Divine mercies.

In all their afflictions, God [too] was afflicted.

And the angel of God's presence saved them.

In God's love and pity were they redeemed.

And God bore them and carried them all the days.

Isaiah 60:7,9
Nitzavim Haftarah

A Prayer

When the rabbis of Pumpeditha left one another, they would say the following: "May the One who gives life to the living give you a long, good, and stable life."

Babylonian Talmud, Yoma 71a

Personal Thoughts and Commitments
for
Self-Renewal This Week

Vayelech: Final Preparations

Deuteronomy 31:1-30

All is foreseen but human beings have free will.

Pirkei Avot 3:19

✔ Like all humans, Moses prepares for his death.

✔ He appoints Joshua as his successor.

✔ He charges the priests to write down the teaching.

Sunday

Joshua is the one who shall cross at your head, as Adonai has spoken.

Deuteronomy 31:3

Things unanticipated are bound to occur. Not everything can be planned, even as you bring order back to your life. Remember you only can control what you can control—and that's not a lot. So plan for the unexpected. The world will continue to spin fast and furious without you at its head. God helps Moses finally to realize it. Take your lead from him.

Monday

And he said unto them: I am a hundred and twenty years old this day; I can no more go out and come in.

Deuteronomy 31:2

Although the Midrash tells us that Moses remained clear-eyed and strong up until and including the day he died, he states here that he no longer can attend to the rigorous demands of leadership. Because he is tired of it? Because God has decreed that now is his time to die? We are not told.

The former is no less respectable a reason for stepping down than the latter. It takes a certain wisdom to recognize when we have reached our limit. Clinging stubbornly to old behavior patterns long after they have outlived their usefulness is the kind of behavioral loop that practically defines addiction.

In the parlance of recovery fellowships, "going out" means going back to our quick fix of choice and "coming in" means entering recovery. What did it take for us, personally, to reach the point where we realized we could no longer "go out and come in," when we were ready to finally and fully make a commitment to staying in? Maybe what it took was that awful "hundred-and-twenty-years-old feeling," when we were hurting, decrepit, and near death. The point, as has often been said, when we got sick and tired of being sick and tired. Thank God, we can keep that sorry point behind us. And yet . . . if it helps keep our recovery alive another day, then it is truly *zichron livrachah*—"a memory for a blessing."

Tuesday

**On the day of death, one considers one's life as if
it had been only a single day.**
Zohar I, 98b

As children, life seems like an eternity. As we grow older, the days seem to fleet by like falling stars. That's why it is most important to live a repentant life—we never know when it will end. And remember to tell those whom you love that you *do* love them! These moments of shared intimacy transcend even the transient moment of death.

Wednesday

Rejoice in your lot and enjoy what little you have.
Derech Eretz Zuta 3

Not an easy thing to do. We seem to be driven to want more because we are dissatisfied with what we have, acknowledging that we don't really have much. The truth is that the material world is not much, anyway. It is time that is so precious—and sharing it with those we love. Be happy with what you have, because it is you who has it. And share it with others. Less is truly more.

Thursday

Assemble the people, the men and the women and the little ones . . .
Deuteronomy 31:12

Here, at last, is one place in the Torah where men, women, and children are specifically and equally referred to for the commandment of assembling every seven years, at Sukkot, to hear the king read the entire Torah. Clearly, this action is intended to recreate the Revelation at Sinai: the Jews, united again; the Torah spoken before the multitude once more—all in testament of the God of Abraham, the God of Isaac, the God of Jacob.

God doesn't change, but we do. Different things matter to us as we grow. We move on with our lives, but we need to remember where we came from and who we are. And, just as recovery unifies us internally, so can it bring us closer to the people in our lives. We are more loving, more lovable, and more aware of the common bonds that connect us all. As the Yiddish proverb puts it, "Living is with people." We can't recover alone.

Both the Torah and the Twelve Steps emphasize passing on the tradition: the Torah, to our children; the Twelve Steps, to the newcomer. On the Great Sabbath before Passover, when there is a feeling of impending redemption in the air, we read the following words from the last prophet, Malachi (3:24): "And he shall turn the heart of the parents to the children, and the heart of the children to their parents." People united for a good cause, relationships restored—that, too, is Torah.

Friday

Write down this poem and teach it to the people of Israel; put it in their mouths in order that this poem may be My witness against the people of Israel.
Deuteronomy 31:19

A life of Torah is poetry. It speaks of our faith in God and in ourselves. It is also our guarantor for the future—that there may be a future.

Shabbat

**Be strong and resolute. Be not fearful or in dread
of them. God Godself marches with you. God
will not fail or forsake you.**

Deuteronomy 31:6

Some may see faith and personal strength as a contradiction
in terms. How can one rely on self when the source of
strength is God? Consider your faith. Dig deeply. Ours is not
a faith that demands abdication of self. We do not lose ourselves in God. Instead we find ourselves in God. Judaism is a
partnership between God and the Jewish people. It is through
that partnership, that covenant established on the fiery
mountaintop of Sinai, that one draws personal strength to
face the challenges of daily living. Our people faced challenges from the time our nation was born. Our ancestors rose
from the oppression of slavery, because God beckoned them
to return to the Promised Land. Moses led the people, but it
was the people who took the journey, who walked through
the desert for forty years. That takes strength and courage. It
takes vision and a desire to realize the dream.

Your journey in recovery is like the journey in the desert.
God continues to beckon to this day: Don't be afraid. Return
to Me and be returned. Set out on the path, and I will help
you on your way.

The path is hard. That's where faith and personal courage
come in. Especially when your personal strength wanes, your
faith takes up the slack. The self is potentially strong; we
were created *be'tzelem Elohim,* in the image of God.

Make preparations for your journey. Whether you have just
started it or have been walking for a long time, final preparations are always necessary. It's not what you are going to do
that matters. However elusive the end may be, and you may
never get there, it's the final preparations that shape our journey. It's getting where we are going, not reaching our final
destination.

Questions for Self-Reflection

1. In preparation for my eventual death, have I left behind lasting values, written them down for others to read?

2. Have I been open with others and told those I love how I really feel about life?

3. Has my life been an open book, or is it sealed with my life?

Notes to Myself

Sacred Thoughts for Holy Living

Everyone carries with them at least one and probably many pieces to someone else's puzzle. Sometimes they know it. Sometimes they don't. And when you present your piece which is worthless to you, to another, whether you know it or not, you are a messenger from the Most High.

Rabbi Lawrence Kushner

For Recovery, A Hymn

Return O Israel to Adonai your God

For you have stumbled in your iniquity.

Take with you words

And return to Adonai.

Whoever is wise, let him understand these things.

Whoever is prudent, let him know them

For the ways of Adonai are right

And the just walk in them.

But the transgressors stumble.

Hosea 14:2-3a, 10
Shabbat Shuvah Haftarah

A Prayer

Praised are You, God, who has not turned away my prayer or faithful care from me.

Psalm 66:20

Personal Thoughts and Commitments
for
Self-Renewal This Week

Haazinu: A Song of the Heart
Deuteronomy 32:1-52

Shiru lAdonai shir chadash.
Sing unto God a new song.
Psalm 96:1

✔ At the border of the Promised Land, Moses sings a song of hope for the people he has led, which reflects his faith in God.

✔ Moses' final instruction urges the people to follow the straight path on which they have journeyed over the past forty years.

✔ Then Moses goes up Mount Nebo to prepare for his death.

Sunday

Remember the days of old. Consider the years of ages past. Ask your parents, they will inform you. Your elders, they will tell you.
Deuteronomy 32:7

The life of the Jewish people is a sacred book. The lives of our families are woven through history in the pages of that sacred book. It is our book, because each day we live, our lives are recorded in it as well. Live a life you want recorded. Let the song in your heart be of one melody with your people.

Monday

**My doctrine shall drop as the rain, my speech
shall distill like the dew . . .**
Deuteronomy 32:2

At the outset of one of the most poetic passages in the Torah,
Moses likens the Torah to rain. What a beautiful metaphor!
Just as water is vital to sustain life, so does Torah sustain the
Jewish spirit. Just as rain comes from above, so does Torah
come from the Highest Power. And, just as rain cleans and
purifies, so does Torah.

We need both water and recovery every day. Rabbi Israel
Salanter used to say, "True, the mouth is said to be as far
away from the heart as heaven is from earth, but we all know
that when rain drops down from heaven, it causes things to
grow on earth." Slowly, gradually . . . growth happens a little
bit at a time—in steps.

From the same crystal-clear pool of thought, the prophet
Isaiah said, "For as the rain and snow come from heaven,
and return not there but soak the earth and make it bring
forth vegetation . . . so it is with the word that comes out of
My mouth, it does not come back to me with its task
undone" (55:8, 10, 11).

Where we have been has helped get us to where we are today.
We are all part of the plan, but that doesn't mean that we
always have to "go with the flow." The Torah teaches that
there is a moral order that transcends the natural order. The
firstborn is not always foremost. "Loser" can win. Today, let
us ask for the wisdom to know which battles are worth fight-
ing and which are better to let go.

Tuesday

**The purity of the thought in the heart is
recognized by the words on the lips.**
Zohar V, 295

You are more than what you say. The essential you is
expressed through what you do and say. And if that's not
who you really are, then change what you do and say. But the
real intention of what you do is sealed in the heart. Let it
flow forth to your lips so that others may hear the sweet
melody of your soul. Sing it out, loud and clear.

Wednesday

Humans look with their eyes, but God looks into the heart.
1 Samuel 16:7

That's the difference between being human and being divine.
But we can learn from God. Don't be deceived by what you
see with your eyes. Look beyond the pretty face, the exquisite
facade of body. Consider the soul instead. That's the way others are looking at you, as well. And as for God, God is
peering into your heart. What will God find there?

Thursday

**The Rock. Your work is perfect; for all Your
ways are justice.**

Deuteronomy 32:4

When we are most at peace with ourselves, when our hearts
are fully open to the many blessings before us, there is a certain joyous *rightness* about the world, a profound sense of
meaning, purpose, and a Greater Presence. The universe itself
seems to rhyme—"and we saw that it was good."

But at the other end of the emotional spectrum is despair. Life
itself seems pointless. We find it hard to accept the pain and
catastrophes that life inevitably brings. God has let us down.
Reconciling God's "perfect work" to life's cruel blows is one
of our most difficult tests of faith.

Rabbi Abraham J. Twerski offers the following analogy:
When a toddler is given a shot, the doctor may ask the mother to help hold the struggling child down. The child does not
understand nor care that the injection is for her own good—
she only knows that it hurts. In fact, her pain is probably
sharpened by the perceived "betrayal" of her mother. And
yet, as soon as the doctor is through, whom does the little
one first turn to for comfort?

God is that mother, God is that doctor, and God is that Rock.
Sometimes the ship of our own will and expectations is
dashed to pieces upon it, sometimes we cling to it for dear life
with the desperation of a shipwreck survivor, but it is always
there. And perfect.

Friday

**Take to heart all the words with which I have warned you
this day. Enjoin them on your children so that they may
faithfully fulfill all the terms of this teaching.**

Deuteronomy 32:46

All that you do with your life is a teaching. If you want others who come after you to benefit from what you have
learned by experience, then teach your children and all those
around you. Tell them what your addiction did to your life
and how your recovery has renewed that life.

Shabbat

**This is not a trifling thing for you; it is your very life.
Through it you shall long endure on the land which you are
about to occupy upon crossing the Jordan.**

Deuteronomy 32:47

Every time the Israelites stand poised, ready to enter the
Promised Land, they have to be reminded of their obligation.
If you want to live and live long on the land which God has
promised to you and your children, then you'd better journey
on the right path. It's no simple thing. It's hard work to stay
clean, to stay sober, to live a decent life. Temptations sur-
round us. But Torah has the potential of changing your
whole life. And that is more tempting than alcohol, drugs,
food, money, or sex.

Sometimes Twelve Step programs seem to occupy our whole
lives. We want to tell the world about our recovery. We may
even feel more attached to our fellowship than we do to the
Jewish community in which we live. It's OK to feel that way.
If recovery does not remain our first priority, then it is likely
that we will not remain in recovery. Yet, recovery is only a
basis for a healthier, happier life. It is not life itself. Sure, we
will want to "practice these principles in all our affairs," as
Step Twelve suggests. But eventually we do have to move
back into our community—and change it if necessary. Our
very presence in that community changes it. But on Shabbat
we don't look to change the world in which we live. It is the
one day of the week during which we are reminded that we
are not the Creator, we are merely the created ones. So, for
twenty-four hours, just sit back and let God's special Shabbat
world transform you. You'll be glad you did and certainly be
ready to sing that song that has been welling up in your heart
for years. Let it become a new Shabbat melody, a sweet
psalm to your ears.

Questions for Self-Reflection

1. How can I sing out the joy that I feel in my heart?

2. How does my faith in God elevate all that I do?

3. What can I do to lead others in the path that I have taken?

Notes to Myself

Sacred Thoughts for Holy Living

The whole world is nothing more than a singing and dancing before the Holy Blessed One. Every Jew is a singer before God, and every letter of the Torah is a musical note.

Nathan ben Naftali Herz

For Recovery, A Hymn

My child, listen to my words.
Incline your ear toward what I have to say.
Do not let them depart from your eyes.
Keep them in the midst of your heart.
For they are life for those who find them
And health to all flesh.
Above all that you guard, keep your heart
For out of it are the issues of life.

Proverbs 4:20-23

A Prayer

Source of Mercy
With loving strength
Untie our tangles.

Your chanting folk
Raise high, make pure.
Accept our song.

Like Your own eye
Lord, keep us safe
Who union seek.

Cleanse and bless us,
Infuse us ever with loving care.

From "Ana Be'koach"
by Zalman Schacter-Shalomi
in Hashir Ve'hashevach

Personal Thoughts and Commitments
for
Self-Renewal This Week

Vezot Ha'berachah:
The Blessing . . . of Recovery

Deuteronomy 33:1-34:12

Humans were created to learn wisdom.

Abraham ibn Ezra on Job 5:21

✔ In the tradition of those who came before him, Moses blesses the people before his death.

✔ The death of Moses is both end and beginning. Moses dies, and the Israelites begin their entry into the Promised Land as a free people under the leadership of Joshua.

Simchat Torah

Happy are You, O Israel, who is like you?
A people saved by Adonai . . .

Deuteronomy 33:29

Rabbi Joseph Hertz calls the Jewish people "a unique people, in the care of a unique God." Prior to putting the Twelve Steps into our lives, many of us thought that we were "terminally unique." No one could *possibly* understand our problems or identify with the pain of being us. Ironically, that sense of being hopelessly isolated was itself a substantial part of the pain. And our attempts to fix it, self-administered (of course!), proved progressively ineffective and increasingly terminal.

We entered a fellowship and, lo and behold, discovered that there were others like us . . . from all backgrounds. Even some Jews. That in itself was a great relief. Part of the blessing and joy of recovery is having similarly crazy people to have fun and commiserate with, people who can share and thus can accept the aspect of us (and our past) that still remains socially unacceptable.

Another reason to be grateful is that we are here at all. We in recovery are very much "a people saved by God." We tried real hard to self-destruct, but it didn't work. Someone Else had other plans. This is not to minimize the personal effort and willingness it takes to remain in recovery—just to acknowledge the help that we've received along the way, the help that got us here.

As Jews, as recovering people, we need never again be alone in our suffering . . . or unwilling to console the pain of others. Despite our differences, we have forged bonds that will endure as long as we let them. Those who have wept and laughed together are no longer strangers.

And there has not risen a prophet since in Israel like unto Moses.
Deuteronomy 34:10

The great Hasidic master, Rabbi Zusya, used to say: "When I come to the next world, no one will ask me why I wasn't like Moses. Instead, they will ask me why wasn't I like Zusya— why didn't I live up to what I was capable of?" We don't have to be like anyone else—it is futile even to try—but it's a good idea to direct our efforts towards fulfilling our own unique potential.

We have learned the hard way that we cannot run from ourselves. No matter where you go, there you are again. Recovery's greatest blessing is self-acceptance. We can better accept who we are if we know that we are trying our best to be the best person that we can be.

These are among the final words in the Torah. The completion of each of the Five Books of the Torah is noted in synagogues by the congregation rising to exclaim, *"Chazak, chazak, ve'nitchazek"*—"Be strong, be strong, and let us strengthen each other." Certainly this principle is one of the spiritual cornerstones of recovery.

As is this: Turning it over. Both Torah and recovery are life-long processes. When we get to the end of the Torah scroll, we literally roll it back to the beginning and start anew. Similarly, when one has formally completed the Twelve Steps, it is customary to go back to Step One. Spiritually speaking, every ending is also a beginning. The joy is in the journey . . . one step at a time.

Questions for Self-Reflection

1. Whom should I bless, for I never will know the day that I die?

2. Can I still make my life into a blessing?

3. Am I really ready to enter the Promised Land, even after all these years of wandering?

Notes to Myself

Sacred Thoughts for Holy Living

I remember the friends I made and the jokes I heard and told.

I remember the times when I was able to put up with fools, and the people who were irritating or ungrateful.

I remember the times when they were able to put up with me.

I remember the occasions when the strength of my own courage and generosity surprised others as well as myself.

I remember the times when I dared to think for myself, and found I could be alone.

I remember all that was spontaneous and uncalculating in me, when I seemed to recover the innocence of childhood.

I remember the illnesses from which I was spared, the disasters which never occurred, and my worries about things which never happened.

I remember the moments when I knew I had a soul.

Rabbi Lionel Blue,
From the prayerbook of the Reform Synagogues of Great Britain,
Forms of Prayer for Jewish Worship

For Recovery, A Psalm

I will extol you, Adonai
For You have raised me up.
And have not caused my enemies to rejoice
over me.

Psalm 30:1

A Prayer

May God bless us and keep us.
May God shed Divine light upon us and
be gracious unto us.
May God turn the Divine face to shine
upon Israel and upon all the peoples
of the earth, granting inner peace, the
most precious of all gifts.

Adapted from "Birkat Kohanim,"
the priestly benediction

Afterword

Rabbi Nachman of Bratzlav told of the king who received a disturbing report about the new harvest: Whoever eats of the new crop will be driven mad. The king gathered his counselors and told them: "Since no other food is available, we must eat in order to live. There is nothing else that we can do. But at least let a few of us keep in mind that we are not mad."

It is not among the few that addiction has taken hold in our society. Addiction is not restricted to the poor or the uneducated or the black or the young or the disenfranchised. It is found as well among the affluent and the influential, the white and the mature, women and men. It is not isolated in the ghetto or barrio. Alcohol, marijuana, cocaine, heroin, or PCP—all are equal-opportunity employers.

Addiction is ecumenical. One out of ten Americans is addicted to some substance or another. The same figure applies to Jews. *Tallit* and *tefillin* are no talismans warding off addictive behavior.

Addiction in its multiple guises—the compulsions to gamble, to drink, to smoke, to take drugs, to overeat—is overwhelming. Something deeper than individual idiosyncratic behavior is involved.

What kind of people are we? What kind of culture have we established for our children and our children's children? What values do they take in with the air they breathe? Why do they hurt themselves, oblivious to the consequences? Why do they drink themselves blind, bludgeon their consciousnesses, rip up their flesh with needles, and ingest poisons into their systems? Why, when denied access to the substances, do they rob and steal and kill to support their habits?

My grandmother, no mean psychologist, would say: *Nisht fun kein naches*—"not from joy." These men, women, and children are in pain. They feel poor—and no trust or will or bank deposit can overcome their sense of impoverishment. They feel bored—and no cruise or vacation can overcome the nausea. They feel empty—and no amount of food can fill the vacuum. They feel worthless—and no number of titles and awards can raise their stature. They feel anxious, awkward, nervous—and no amount of liquor or drugs can overcome their self-doubts.

Why are they so many, and why do they come from all walks of life? Why are they so easily hurt, so quickly discouraged, so readily bored with living? They are raised in an enveloping hedonistic culture that prepares the soil for addiction. It is a mass culture rooted in an unstated theology, a popular system of belief more pervasive and more influential among more people than any of the established religions. And like every religion, it is a belief system that teaches what is real and what is phony, what gives meaning and what turns us off to life. Its presuppositions are summed up in its two imperatives: Pursue pleasure and avoid pain.

Hedonism is a system not boldly and publicly articulated these days but, nonetheless, widely and privately held. Hedonism presents itself as offering the unvarnished truth. Conventional preachments call for sacrifice, commitment, pain, and struggle to achieve salvation. Hedonism is neither moralistic nor hypocritical. It whispers to us that all the appeals to self-denial, altruism, idealism, commitment, and martyrdom are deceiving; that while these would have us believe that salvation is something rare, something hard, something to be received at some other time or place, hedonism tells us the naked truth: What we desire is pleasure now and the avoidance of all pain, and this is achievable.

Hedonistic wisdom promises liberation from a world of imperatives, duties, obligations. Flow with natural desires. Put aside your Bibles and prayerbooks. Live your life without sadness or sorrow or martyrdom or disappointment or defeat. Admit to yourself that hedonism is the desire and the end of salvation.

The hedonistic message seems to have a simple, sincere honesty. Who doesn't want pleasure? And who would not avoid pain? The pleasure of love and family and friendship; the pleasures of creativity and aesthetics. Hedonism gets to the core of our reality, our basic human needs, and cuts through the moralism and demands of traditional faiths.

But for all its claims to "tell it like it is," hedonism is seductively misleading and dangerously naive. Hedonism is the stuff that feeds the addictive personality. For, second thought makes it clear that nothing we want in our lives, nothing we regard as valuable, nothing of worth and significance can be gotten without pain, struggle, sacrifice, suffering.

What do we want and what is valuable in our lives? And what can be gained without suffering? Do we want to love and be loved?

He came to me, this man, with his doubts and asked in all seriousness, "How do I know if I love her?" I answered: "Are you willing to sacrifice for her sake, to suffer with her? If you answer 'yes,' it is a sign of love, but if you answer 'no,' it means that here there is no love." To love and be loved requires compatibility and compassion, from the Latin meaning "to bear, to suffer." Whoever loves a spouse, a child, a parent, a friend, opens himself or herself up to pain. Vulnerability is the price we pay for love's wonders. Does not to love and be loved by a child mean that there is never a moment as long as we live when we stop worrying about that child? To love and be loved by parents—those whose names we cry out in the black night when we are feverish and alone, parents who someday will cry out our name, reversing their parental roles with us—does not such love demand responsiveness, suffering, and reciprocity? No one can hurt us more than those we love.

And so with friendship. Can we have a friend or be a friend without offering some sacrifice of self? Where is friendship more truly tested than when deprivation and sacrifice is called for? Who will hear the confession of our errors and not condemn, who will contain our fears, who will add their blood to our own? Is there *anything* we want, anything that brings us joy, that is immune to suffering and pain?

And so with creativity. Can we write an essay, compose a song, paint a picture, play an instrument, run a race without pain?

Hedonism misrepresents real living. Against the illusions of hedonism, Judaism presents us with an unflinching Reality Principle. Cast out of the Garden of Eden into the real world,

Eve is told by God the principle of life: "With pain and travail shalt thou bring forth children." No birth without sacrifice. In your blood, Eve, you give life to the world. And to Adam, God spoke reality: "In the sweat of thy face shalt you eat bread till thou return into the ground, for out of the earth wast thou taken; for dust art thou and unto dust shalt thou return."

The myth opens the innocent eyes of Adam and Eve to the real world, east of Eden. Pain is the companion of birth. Pain is the companion of growth. The whole of life is nothing but the process of giving birth to oneself. To live and to love, to create and to work, one must be willing to suffer. One must be willing to rip thorns and thistles from the earth's growth and wrestle with God's angels and rise up limping lame. To give birth to your own self is to endure anguish. Life is filled with births and deaths, with attachments and separations.

So hedonism couples two ideas—the pursuit of pleasure and the avoidance of pain—that turn out to be contradictory. Jewish wisdom knows that spiritual, cultural, aesthetic, creative pleasures cannot be achieved without pain.

When hedonism is caught in the lie, it holds out a heavier dose of enticements. If the pleasures we seek are too painful to accomplish, if it requires too great an effort to master a talent or to transform the perverseness of society, if the desire of our hearts is too high or too heavy to achieve, then drop them for pleasures that come without pain. If love requires commitment, if the struggle involves blood, sweat, and tears, then let go of the ideals. Relax, play it cool, don't let things bug you. Take the short cut, grab hold of easy, quick, immediate sensations. Eat and drink, suck the juices of easy joy. Feed the body. There is pleasure enough in good food, good wine, good sex. If the self aspires to higher things, redefine your self.

From infancy we are raised to fear pain, to stop the headache instantly. And we have found the cure, the technological panacea. Open up the sacred chest—medicine cabinet—the *Aron Kodesh* of our homes, and behold a pharmacopia of potions and pills promising salvation. Amphetamines and barbiturates, stimulants and sedatives: "Cause us Adonai to lie down in peace and raise us up again unto life." Thy miracles are daily with us "evening, morn, and noon."

As we pressure the pharmacist for soporifics, we pressure our religious institutions and leaders to write quick prescriptions, easy answers, ritual routines that will help us escape from the pains of life. Prescriptions and proscriptions faithfully followed by rote will help us avoid the exertions of thinking, the wrestlings of conscience, the struggles to create convictions out of ambiguities.

The addict comes in many forms. Gambler, overeater, alcoholic, sexaholic, drugaholic, workaholic, cultaholic. But in all, there is an underlying desire to escape reality, its ambiguities, conflicts, and cruelties. By pouring oneself into a single activity or obsession, the addict hopes to block out the world.

A word about the workaholic, the most acceptable addict in our culture. The person addictively drawn to something vaguely called "career," whose compulsion may be called "upward mobility," is no less escapist than the substance abuser. She is as dependent as the others. She is drunk with mirthless sobriety. He is intoxicated with the cold efficiency of the computer. He seeks escape from the affective world of personal relationships. She mocks at community service, at everything that cannot be summed up with the bottom line. She has no time or room for poetry or philosophy or religion or family or friends. The workaholic has no time and no interest in the struggle for ideals or idealism or personal service. He will pay someone else to meditate for him, to parent for him, or to engage the world for him. Annoyed, he will cheerlessly write out a check to avoid the pain of involvement. Only let him alone to feed his accounts.

Hedonism is the religion of our mass culture. Hedonism is an idolatry. The addict is an idolater who has found his small gods and has blocked out the larger God. He has chosen his compulsions and denied his freedom. She has consciously decided not to live. Afraid of pain, she has deadened her sensibilities. Fearful of dependence and the responsibilities and pains it entails, she has become dependent on something or someone other and less than self.

Hedonism lies to us. It insists that all we want out of life is the presence of pleasure and the absence of pain. But that is untrue. Who would allow a frontal lobotomy to be performed on himself, an incision severing nerve fibers in the brain, which would deaden all pains, all fears, all concerns? Who of us would allow the implantation of electrodes connected to the pleasure centers of the brain, bombarding us with ceaseless pleasures, requiring from us no struggle, providing a life of immediate and constant gratification until we die by exhaustion?

We would not choose to be chained to a pleasure machine devoid of pain because a life without aspiration, ideals, or purpose is euthanasia. To live is to know that you are mandated, that there is something significant that you must do, something purposive that offers meaning to your life and therefore something deserving of your suffering. To be alive is to know that you are a child of imperatives. As Micah summed it up, "It has been told thee what is good and what is required of you: to do justice, to love mercy, and to walk humbly with thy God." None of these imperatives can be realized without struggle, pain, and sacrifice.

Therein lies human dignity, self-respect, and meaning. No one chooses suffering for its own sake. We choose life and love and peace and justice. But no one can truthfully choose those ennobling ideals without embracing struggle as well. Therefore wisdom counsels: See to it that what you live for is worthy of sacrifice. Only the dead have no imperatives, no *mitzvot*. As the Talmud puts it, "When a person dies, that person is freed from Torah and *mitzvot*, from study and deeds of goodness" (Shabbat 30a). The dead are beyond pain and beyond life.

We Jews do not seek pain. There is no masochism in our tradition. But we know that to feel no pain is to court disaster. Not to feel pain is far more dangerous than to feel pain.

We live in a culture founded on a dangerously false understanding of reality, one that prepares the ground for addiction. Its lure is a painless life, but its price is death.

This pain-avoiding hedonistic culture has affected the upbringing of our children. When parents will not allow children to visit the sick relative in the hospital or attend the funeral of their grandmother lest they see human beings cry or mourn their loss, they rob the children of their humanity and prepare them for the perpetual search for painkillers. Their character is spoiled in parental overprotection that reduces life to the avoidance of unpleasantness and the pursuit of proximate pleasure.

Hedonism whispers, "Choose, please." Judaism advises, "Choose life." The two are not synonymous. We must not deprive ourselves or our children of the right to struggle, the capacity to suffer, the courage to endure pain, or the mandate to afflict our souls. To be Jewish is to prepare to struggle, to combat those who step on the throats of the innocent, to love and care for each other. To be Jewish is to bear with dignity the scars and blemishes that give meaning to our lives.

Hedonism has nothing to live for—only a life to avoid. In heroin, heroism is denied.

It is not enough to tell our children to "just say no." They will not say "no" to drugs and not go back on their word until they learn to say "yes" to life. And to say "yes" to life is to say "yes" to the pain and struggle and sacrifice without which no ideal can be touched. God is called "the life of the universe." Alive, God does not sit above the clouds in holy indifference. Alive, God too feels and suffers and is afflicted in our afflictions. "For a long time I have kept silence, I have kept still and restrained Myself; now I will cry out like a woman in travail, I will gasp and pain" (Isaiah 42:14). As God lives, we are alive. As God lives and struggles, so must we who would live.

Rabbi Harold M. Schulweis

Weekly Calendar of Torah Readings[1]

GENESIS	1992/93	1993/94	1994/95	1995/96	1996/97
BEREISHIT	Oct 18	Oct 8	Sept 25	Oct 15	Oct 6
NOACH	Oct 25	Oct 10	Oct 2	Oct 22	Oct 13
LECH LECHA	Nov 1	Oct 17	Oct 9	Oct 29	Oct 20
VAYERA	Nov 8	Oct 24	Oct 16	Nov 5	Oct 27
CHAYEI SARAH	Nov 15	Oct 31	Oct 23	Nov 12	Nov 3
TOLDOT	Nov 22	Nov 7	Oct 30	Nov 19	Nov 10
VAYETZE	Nov 29	Nov 14	Nov 6	Nov 26	Nov 17
VAYISHLACH	Dec 6	Nov 21	Nov 13	Dec 3	Nov 24
VAYESHEV	Dec 13	Nov 28	Nov 20	Dec 10	Nov 31
MIKETZ	Dec 20	Dec 5	Nov 27	Dec 17	Dec 8
VAYIGASH	Dec 27	Dec 12	Dec 4	Dec 24	Dec 15
VAYECHI	Jan 3	Dec 19	Dec 11	Dec 31	Dec 22

EXODUS

	1992/93	1993/94	1994/95	1995/96	1996/97
SHEMOT	Jan 10	Dec 18	Dec 18	Jan 7	Dec 29
VAERA	Jan 17	Dec 25	Dec 25	Jan 14	Jan 5
BO	Jan 24	Jan 9	Jan 1	Jan 21	Jan 12
BESHALLACH	Jan 31	Jan 16	Jan 8	Jan 28	Jan 19
YITRO	Feb 7	Jan 23	Jan 15	Feb 4	Jan 26
MISHPATIM	Feb 14	Jan 30	Jan 22	Feb 11	Feb 2
TERUMAH	Feb 21	Feb 6	Jan 29	Feb 18	Feb 9
TETZAVEH	Feb 28	Feb 13	Feb 5	Feb 25	Feb 16
KI TISA	Mar 7	Feb 20	Feb 12	Mar 3	Feb 23
VAYAKHEL	Mar 14	Feb 27	Feb 19	Mar 10	Mar 2
PEKUDEI	Mar 14	Mar 6	Feb 26	Mar 27	Mar 9

LEVITICUS

	1992/93	1993/94	1994/95	1995/96	1996/97
VAYIKRA	Mar 21	Mar 13	Mar 5	Mar 24	Mar 16
TZAV	Mar 28	Mar 20	Mar 12	Mar 31	Mar 23
SHEMINI	Apr 11	Apr 3	Mar 19	Apr 7	Mar 30
TAZRIA	Apr 18	Apr 10	Mar 26	Apr 14	Apr 6
METZORA	Apr 18	Apr 10	Apr 2	Apr 14	Apr 13
ACHAREI MOT	Apr 25	Apr 17	Apr 23	Apr 21	Apr 27
KEDOSHIM	Apr 25	Apr 17	Apr 30	Apr 21	May 4
EMOR	May 2	Apr 24	May 7	Apr 28	May 11
BEHAR	May 9	May 1	May 14	May 5	May 18
BECHUKOTAI	May 9	May 1	May 21	May 5	May 25

NUMBERS

	1992/93	1993/94	1994/95	1995/96	1996/97
BEMIDBAR	May 16	May 8	May 28	May 12	Jun 1
NASO	May 23	May 15	Jun 4	May 19	Jun 8
BEHAALOTECHA	May 30	May 22	Jun 11	May 26	Jun 15
SHELACH LECHA	Jun 6	May 29	Jun 18	Jun 9	Jun 22
KORACH	Jun 13	Jun 5	Jun 25	Jun 16	Jun 29
CHUKAT	Jun 20	Jun 12	Jul 2	Jun 23	Jul 6
BALAK	Jun 27	Jun 19	Jul 9	Jun 23	Jul 13
PINCHAS	Jul 4	Jun 26	Jul 16	Jun 30	Jul 20
MATTOT	Jul 11	Jul 3	Jul 23	Jul 7	Jul 27
MASEI	Jul 11	Jul 3	Jul 23	Jul 7	Jul 27

Weekly Calendar of Torah Readings

DEUTERONOMY	1992/93	1993/94	1994/95	1995/96	1996/97
DEVARIM	Jul 18	Jul 10	Jul 30	Jul 14	Aug 3
VA'ETCHANAN	Jul 25	Jul 17	Aug 6	Jul 21	Aug 10
EKEV	Aug 1	Jul 24	Aug 13	Jul 28	Aug 17
RE'EH	Aug 8	Jul 31	Aug 20	Aug 4	Aug 24
SHOFTIM	Aug 15	Aug 7	Aug 27	Aug 11	Aug 31
KI TETZE	Aug 22	Aug 14	Sept 3	Aug 18	Sept 7
KI TAVO	Aug 29	Aug 21	Sept 10	Aug 25	Sept 14
NITZAVIM	Sept 5	Aug 28	Sept 17	Sept 1	Sept 21
VAYELECH	Sept 5	Sept 4	Sept 24	Sept 1	Sept 21
HAAZINU	Sept 12	Sept 11	Oct 1	Sept 15	Sept 28
VEZOT HA'BERACHAH	Oct 8	Sept 28	Oct 17	Oct 6	Oct 24

[1] The dates listed reflect the first day of the week during which the weekly portion is read, beginning with Saturday evening. This chart does not take into account holiday or Rosh Chodesh readings. For Vezot Ha'berachah, the date listed is for Simchat Torah specifically (one day earlier in most Reform synagogues). In cases where the Hebrew calendar requires an adjustment through the doubling of portions, the date is repeated two weeks in a row.

About the Authors

RABBI KERRY M. OLITZKY, D.H.L. is Director of the School of Education at Hebrew Union College-Jewish Institute of Religion in New York City. As such, he also directs its Doctor of Ministry Program and has been a trendsetter in developing training programs for clergy and other professionals, especially in the area of addiction and chemical dependency. Rabbi Olitzky is the author of numerous books and articles, including (with Stuart Copans, M.D.) *Twelve Jewish Steps to Recovery: A Personal Guide to Turning from Alcoholism and Other Addictions* (Jewish Lights Publishing, 1991). He is also the producer/moderator of *Message of Israel* (ABC Radio Network).

AARON Z. is a recovering person, who is active in his synagogue and the chairperson of his area's JACS (Jewish Alcoholics, Chemically Dependent Persons and Significant Others) Foundation meeting. He is a self-employed writer who lives in the Greater New York area with his wife and three children. He shares his experiences and insights into recovery and Torah in the spirit of the Twelfth Step and, in the writing of this book, has gratefully grown in both.

SHARON M. STRASSFELD is co-author of the popular *Jewish Catalog* series. These innovative "how to" books continue to provide all people with ways to enrich their lives.

RABBI HAROLD M. SCHULWEIS of Temple Valley Beth Shalom in Encino, California, is widely recognized as an innovative and inspiring religious educator. His work has been especially sen-sitive to the dilemmas and struggles of contemporary life.

About the Art

The cover art and ornamentation of this book are from artist MATY GRÜNBERG's striking portfolio of the twelve gates of the Old City of Jerusalem. This art emphasizes the relationship between heavenly and earthly in all our lives through the prism of Jerusalem.

Grünberg is an Israeli artist who has made his home in London since the late 1960s. His illuminated books and sculptures are found in the collections of museums and institutions throughout the world.

About JEWISH LIGHTS Publishing

People of all faiths and backgrounds yearn for books that attract, engage, educate and spiritually inspire.

Our principal goal is to stimulate thought and help all people learn about who the Jewish People are, where they come from, and what the future can be made to hold. While people of our diverse Jewish heritage are the primary audience, our books speak to the Christian world as well and will broaden their understanding of Judaism and the roots of their own faith.

We bring to you authors who are at the forefront of spiritual thought and experience. While each has something different to say, they all say it in a voice that you can hear.

Our books are designed to welcome you and then to engage, stimulate and inspire. We judge our success not only by whether or not our books are beautiful and commercially successful, but by whether or not they make a difference in your life.

We at Jewish Lights take great care to produce beautiful books that present meaningful spiritual content in a form that reflects the art of making high quality books. Therefore, we want to acknowledge those who contributed to the production of this book.

Art Direction and Production
Rachel Kahn

Art
Maty Grünberg

Cover Design
Nancy Malerba, Weathersfield, Vermont

Type
Set in Mistral, Sabon, and Optima
Barbara Homeyer Type, Inc., Lebanon, New Hampshire

Cover Printing
New England Book Components, Hingham, Massachusetts

Printing and Binding
Book Press, Inc., Brattleboro, Vermont

Motivation, Inspiration & Consolation for Recovery

RENEWED EACH DAY
Daily Twelve Step Recovery Meditations Based on the Bible
VOLUME I: Genesis & Exodus
by *Rabbi Kerry M. Olitzky & Aaron Z.*
Introduction by *Rabbi Michael A. Signer*
Afterword by JACS Foundation

Using a seven day/weekly guide format, a recovering person and a spiritual leader who is reaching out to addicted people, reflect on the traditional weekly Bible reading. They bring strong spiritual support for daily living and recovery from addictions of all kinds: alcohol, drugs, eating, gambling and sex. A profound sense of the religious spirit soars through their words and brings all people in Twelve Step recovery programs home to a rich and spiritually enlightening tradition.

"Meets a vital need; it offers a chance for people turning from alcoholism and addiction to renew their spirits and draw upon the Jewish tradition to guide and enrich their lives."
—*Rabbi Irving (Yitz) Greenberg*, President, CLAL,
The National Jewish Center for Learning and Leadership

"Will benefit anyone familiar with a 'religion of the Book.' Jews, Christians, Muslims. . . ."
—*Ernest Kurtz,* author of *Not-God: A History of Alcoholics Anonymous* & *The Spirituality of Imperfection*

6"x 9", 224 pp. Quality Paperback, ISBN 1-879045-12-5   **$12.95**

RENEWED EACH DAY
Daily Twelve Step Recovery Meditations Based on the Bible
VOLUME II: Leviticus, Numbers & Deuteronomy
by *Rabbi Kerry M. Olitzky & Aaron Z.*
Introduction by *Sharon M. Strassfeld*
Afterword by *Rabbi Harold M. Schulweis*

"An enduring impact upon the faith community as it seeks to blend the wisdom of the ages represented in the tradition with the twelve steps to recovery and wholeness."
—*Robert H. Albers, Ph.D., Editor,* Journal of Ministry in Addiction & Recovery

"A most valuable contribution to those seeking strength from our tradition in the struggle to move beyond addiction."—*Rabbi Hillel Friedman,* Executive Director,
Department on Religious Affairs, United Jewish Appeal/Federation

6"x 9", 280 pp. Quality Paperback, ISBN 1-879045-13-3   **$14.95**

> **Available as a beautiful slipcased two-volume set.**
> 6"x 9", 504 pp. Quality Paperback, ISBN 1-879045-21-4   **$27.90**

AN INSPIRING VISUAL REMINDER OF COMMITMENT TO RECOVERY

The Jerusalem Gates Portfolio

by Maty Grünberg

Twelve beautiful prints of illustrations from

Twelve Jewish Steps To Recovery

Artist Maty Grünberg's striking illustrations of the gates of the Old City of Jerusalem emphasize the relationship between heavenly and earthly in all of our lives through the prism of this city, holy to people of all faiths.

- Beautiful 9"x 12" reproductions of twelve original pen and ink drawings by celebrated Israeli artist, Maty Grünberg. Commissioned by the publisher specially for *Twelve Jewish Steps To Recovery*.
- Printed on fine quality acid-free paper.
- Enhanced with key inspiration word printed in a second color.
- Presented as a portfolio of twelve separate prints, each suitable for framing.

$49.95

Rabbi Kerry M. Olitzky & Stuart A. Copans, M.D.

TWELVE JEWISH STEPS TO RECOVERY
A Personal Guide To Turning From Alcoholism & Other Addictions.'....
Drugs, Food, Gambling, Sex

by *Rabbi Kerry M. Olitzky & Stuart A. Copans, MD*
Preface by *Abraham J. Twerski, MD*
Introduction by *Rabbi Sheldon Zimmerman*
Illustrations by *Maty Grünberg*
"Getting Help" by *JACS Foundation*

A Jewish perspective on the Twelve Steps of addiction recovery programs with consolation, inspiration and motivation for recovery. It draws from traditional sources, and quotes from what recovering Jewish people say about their experiences with addictions of all kinds. Inspiring illustrations of the twelve gates of the Old City of Jerusalem.

This book is not just for Jewish people.

It's for all people who would gain strength to heal and insight from Jewish tradition.

- All people who are in trouble with alcohol and drugs and other addictions—food, gambling and sex
- Anyone seeking an understanding of the Twelve Steps from a Jewish perspective—regardless of religious background or affiliation
- Alcoholics and addicts in recovery
- Co-dependents
- Adult children of alcoholics
- Specialists in recovery and treatment

Experts Praise *Twelve Jewish Steps to Recovery*

"Recommended reading for people of all denominations." —*Rabbi Abraham J. Twerski, MD*

"I read *Twelve Jewish Steps* with the eyes of a Christian and came away renewed in my heart. I felt like I had visited my Jewish roots. These authors have deep knowledge of recovery as viewed by Alcoholics Anonymous." —*Rock J. Stack, M.A., L.L. D.*
Manager of Clinical/Pastoral Education, Hazelden Foundation

"This book is the first aimed directly at helping the addicted person and family. Everyone affected or interested should read it." —*Sheila B. Blume, M.D., C.A.C.,*
Medical Director, Alcoholism, Chemical Dependency and Compulsive Gambling Programs,
South Oaks Hospital, Amityville, New York

Readers Praise *Twelve Jewish Steps to Recovery*

"A God-send. Literally. A book from the higher power." —New York, NY
"An excellent, much needed book for the Jewish community." —Coconut Creek, FL
"It's about time such a book has been written." —Rego Park, NY
"Spiritual, sensitive, realistic, helpful." —Tallahassee, FL
"Excellent—changed my life." —Elkhart Lake, WI
"Traditionally Jewish and helpful!" —Monsey, NY
"A book that I've been waiting for." —Berkeley, CA
"Inspiring and reassuring." —Pomona, NJ

6"x 9", 136 pp. Hardcover, ISBN 1-879045-08-7 **$19.95**
6"x 9", 136 pp. Quality Paperback, ISBN 1-879045-09-5 **$12.95**

Other Inspiring Books from Jewish Lights

THE BOOK OF LETTERS
A Mystical Hebrew Alphabet
by *Rabbi Lawrence Kushner*

In calligraphy by the author. Folktales about and exploration of the mystical meanings of the Hebrew Alphabet. Enter a special world of sacred tradition and religious feeling.

• **Popular Hardcover Edition**
6"x 9", 80 pp. Hardcover, two colors, inspiring new Foreword, ISBN 1-879045-00-1 **$24.95**

• **Deluxe Presentation Edition**
9"x 12", 80 pp. Hardcover, four-color text, ornamentation, in a beautiful slipcase
ISBN 1-879045-01-X **$79.95**

• **Collector's Limited Edition**
9"x 12", 80 pp. Hardcover, gold embossed pages, hand assembled slipcase. With silkscreened print.
Limited to 500 signed and numbered copies.
ISBN 1-879045-04-4 **$349.00**

THE RIVER OF LIGHT
Spirituality, Judaism, Consciousness
by *Rabbi Lawrence Kushner*

A manual for all spiritual travelers who would attempt a spiritual journey in our times. Taking us step by step, Kushner allows us to discover the meaning of our own quest: "to allow the river of light—the deepest currents of consciousness—to rise to the surface and animate our lives."

6"x 9", 180 pp. Quality Paperback, ISBN 1-879045-03-6 **$14.95**

THE SPIRIT OF RENEWAL
Crisis & Response in Jewish Life
by *Edward Feld*

"Boldly redefines the landscape of Jewish religious thought after the Holocaust." In order to address the question of faith after the Holocaust, Rabbi Feld places it within the context of responses to great tragedy throughout Jewish history. Poetic. Thought-provoking.

6"x 9", 208 pp. Hardcover, ISBN 1-879045-06-0 **$22.95**

TORMENTED MASTER
The Life and Spiritual Quest of Rabbi Nahman of Bratslav
by *Arthur Green*

Explores the personality and religious quest of Nahman of Bratslav (1772–1810), one of Hasidism's major figures. It unlocks the great themes of spiritual searching that make him a figure of universal religious importance.

6"x 9", 408 pp. Quality Paperback, ISBN 1-879045-11-7 **$17.95**

PUTTING GOD ON THE GUEST LIST
How to Reclaim the Spiritual Meaning of Your Child's Bar or Bat Mitzvah
by *Rabbi Jeffrey K. Salkin*

Helps people find core spiritual values in American Jewry's most misunderstood ceremony —bar and bat mitzvah. In a joining of explanation, instruction and inspiration, Rabbi Salkin helps both parent and child truly *be there* when the moment of Sinai is recreated in their lives.

6"x 9", 184 pp. Hardcover, ISBN 1-879045-20-6 **$21.95**
6"x 9", 184 pp. Quality Paperback, ISBN 1-879045-10-9 **$14.95**

GOD'S PAINTBRUSH
by *Sandy Eisenberg Sasso*
Full color illustrations by *Annette C. Compton*

Through fantasy, involvement and the imagination, *God's Paintbrush* invites children of all faiths and backgrounds to encounter God. For all who wish to cultivate the religious imagination, to encourage children to think and wonder about God. Non-sectarian.

11"x 8$^{1}/_{2}$", 32 pp. Hardcover, Illus. , ISBN 1-879045-22-2 **$15.95**

~Order Information~

Please send me the following book(s):

Copies $ Amount

The Book Of Letters

_____ • Popular Hardcover Edition, $24.95   _____

_____ • Deluxe Presentation Edition, $79.95, plus $5.95 s/h   _____

_____ • Collector's Limited Edition, $349.00, plus $12.50 s/h _____

_____ God Was In This Place And I, i Did Not Know, (hc) $21.95   _____

_____ God's Paintbrush, (hc) $15.95   _____

_____ Honey From The Rock, (pb) $14.95   _____

_____ The Jerusalem Gates Portfolio, $49.95   _____

_____ Putting God On The Guest List, (hc) $21.95   _____

_____ Putting God On The Guest List, (pb) $14.95   _____

_____ Renewed Each Day, Vol I, (pb) $12.95   _____

_____ Renewed Each Day, Vol II, (pb) $14.95   _____

_____ Renewed Each Day, 2-Volume Set, (pb) $27.90   _____

_____ The River Of Light, (pb) $14.95   _____

_____ Seeking The Path To Life, (hc) $19.95   _____

_____ So That Your Values Live On, (hc) $19.95   _____

_____ Spirit Of Renewal, (hc) $22.95   _____

_____ Tormented Master, (pb) $17.95   _____

_____ Twelve Jewish Steps To Recovery, (hc) $19.95   _____

_____ Twelve Jewish Steps To Recovery, (pb) $12.95   _____

For s/h, add $2.95 for the first book, $1 each additional book.   _____

Total _____

~~~ • ~~~

Check enclosed for $_____ *payable to:* JEWISH LIGHTS Publishing.

Charge my credit card: ❑ MasterCard   ❑ Visa   ❑ Discover   ❑ AMEX

Credit Card #_____Expires _____

Name on card _____

Signature_____Phone (_____)_____

Name _____

Street _____

City / State / Zip _____

SHIP TO / GIFT ORDERS: ❑ Same as Above

Name _____

Street _____

City / State / Zip _____

Gift card to read: _____

_____

Phone or mail to: **JEWISH LIGHTS Publishing**
Box 237, Sunset Farm Offices, Route 4, Woodstock, Vermont 05091
Tel **(802) 457-4000**   *Fax* **(802) 457-4004**
Toll free credit card orders **(800) 962-4544** (9AM–5PM EST Monday–Friday)
Generous discounts on quantity orders. Prices subject to change.
Available from better bookstores. Try your bookstore first.
Satisfaction guaranteed

O–RED–1